P9-EAY-003

AFGHANISTAN
in Pictures

Alison Behnke

Lerner Publications Company

Contents

Lerner Publishing Group realizes that current information and statistics quickly become out of date. To extend the usefulness of the Visual Geography Series, we developed www.vgsbooks.com, a website offering links to up-to-date information, as well as in-depth material, on a wide variety of subjects. All of the websites listed on www.vgsbooks.com have been carefully selected by researchers at Lerner Publishing Group. However, Lerner Publishing Group is not responsible for the accuracy or suitability of the material on any website other than <www.lernerbooks.com>. It is recommended that students using the Internet be supervised by a parent or teacher. Links on www.vgsbooks.com will be regularly reviewed and updated as needed.

Copyright © 2003 by Lerner Publications Company

All rights reserved. International copyright secured. No part of this book may be reproduced, stored in a retrieval system, or transmitted in any form or by any means—electronic, mechanical, photocopying, recording, or otherwise—without the prior written permission of Lerner Publications Company, except for the inclusion of brief quotations in an acknowledged review.

Website address: www.lernerbooks.com

Lerner Publications Company
A division of Lerner Publishing Group
241 First Avenue North
Minneapolis, MN 55401 U.S.A.

web enhanced @ www.vgsbooks.com

Library of Congress Cataloging-in-Publication Data

Behnke, Alison.
        Afghanistan in pictures / by Alison Behnke.— Rev. and expanded.
            p.   cm. — (Visual geography series)
        Rev. ed. of: Afghanistan —in pictures / prepared by Geography Department, Lerner Publications
Company.
        Summary: An introduction to the geography, history, government, people, and economy of this
landlocked country with a long history of warfare and conquest.
        Includes bibliographical references and index.
        ISBN: 0-8225-4683-3 (lib. bdg. : alk. paper)
        1. Afghanistan—Juvenile literature. 2. Afghanistan—Pictorial works—Juvenile literature. [1. Afghanistan.]
I. Lerner Publications Company. Geography Dept. Afghanistan in pictures. II. Title. III. Visual geography series
(Minneapolis, Minn.)
DS351.5 .A345 2003
958.1—dc21   2002013613

Manufactured in the United States of America
1 2 3 4 5 6 - JR - 08 07 06 05 04 03

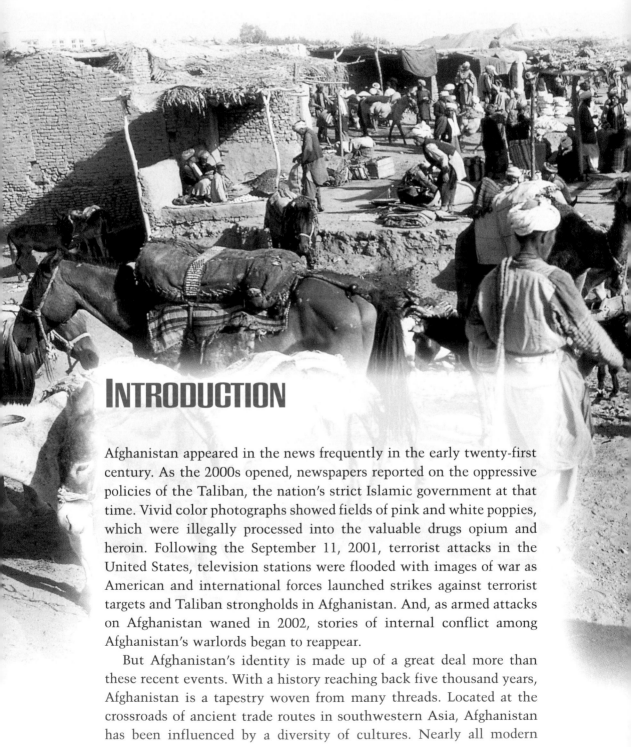

INTRODUCTION

Afghanistan appeared in the news frequently in the early twenty-first century. As the 2000s opened, newspapers reported on the oppressive policies of the Taliban, the nation's strict Islamic government at that time. Vivid color photographs showed fields of pink and white poppies, which were illegally processed into the valuable drugs opium and heroin. Following the September 11, 2001, terrorist attacks in the United States, television stations were flooded with images of war as American and international forces launched strikes against terrorist targets and Taliban strongholds in Afghanistan. And, as armed attacks on Afghanistan waned in 2002, stories of internal conflict among Afghanistan's warlords began to reappear.

But Afghanistan's identity is made up of a great deal more than these recent events. With a history reaching back five thousand years, Afghanistan is a tapestry woven from many threads. Located at the crossroads of ancient trade routes in southwestern Asia, Afghanistan has been influenced by a diversity of cultures. Nearly all modern

Afghans are Muslims (followers of the religion of Islam), but the nation has also been home to followers of Buddhism and other more ancient religions. Artistic and literary traditions in Afghanistan reflect the many cultures that converged on the nation's soil.

At the same time, the country's landlocked location forced it to endure centuries of warfare and conquest. Persians, Greeks, and Mongols were among the groups that sought to stake claims in the region between the 500s B.C. and the A.D. 1500s. The majority of the Afghan people first became part of a unified nation under the leadership of Ahmad Shah Durrani in the 1700s, but more invasions lay ahead. British forces tried to seize control in three Anglo-Afghan wars between 1838 and 1919. A period of peace followed these conflicts, but it ended abruptly with the 1979 invasion of Afghanistan by troops from the Soviet Union. These forces arrived to support Afghanistan's pro-Soviet government, but the event led to the formation of a violent opposition movement. The struggle pitted Soviet soldiers and the Soviet-supported Afghan government against the mujahideen (Islamic warriors).

Millions of Afghans fled to nearby Pakistan and Iran, and thousands of others were killed in the fighting. In 1989 the Soviet Union completely withdrew its troops, and Soviet involvement in Afghanistan ended with the Soviet Union's collapse in 1991. But power struggles and fighting erupted among the mujahideen and continued during the early 1990s. When the Taliban took power in the late 1990s, many mujahideen turned against the fundamentalist regime as it implemented more and more repressive measures. The mujahideen opposition gained international assistance when evidence showed that the Taliban had supported Saudi-born terrorist Osama bin Laden and his al-Qaeda terrorist network, the agents behind the September 11 attacks. An international offensive against the Afghan government forced the Taliban from power in 2001. In June 2002, Hamid Karzai, a relative of one of Afghanistan's former kings, was sworn in as the president of the nation's new government, and the story of Afghanistan took yet another turn.

Just as Afghanistan's history forms an intricate design, the nation's landscape is a pattern of contrasts, from steep mountains and broad deserts to grassy valleys and plains. The fabric of Afghanistan's society, too, is varied. Its people are a diverse mix of ethnicities, with many different physical features, clothing styles, languages, and customs. And while Afghanistan's rich texture has sometimes led to strife, it also provides the country with a wealth of resources and strengths upon which to draw.

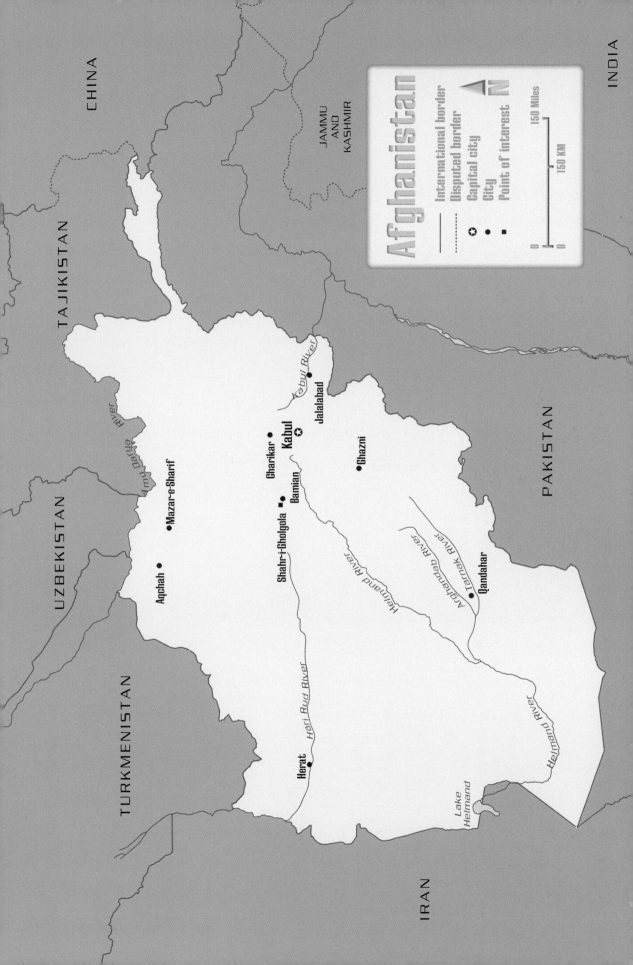

THE LAND

Located near the center of the Asian continent, Afghanistan is a land-locked country. More than half of the nation's harsh but beautiful landscape consists of high plateaus and mountains. Rugged mountain ranges, such as the Hindu Kush, extend across the country. Fertile valleys and plains lie in the northwest, with desert areas in the south.

With 251,773 square miles (652,092 square kilometers) of territory, Afghanistan is slightly smaller than the state of Texas. The former Soviet republics of Turkmenistan, Uzbekistan, and Tajikistan lie to the north. Iran is to the west, and Pakistan is situated to the south and east. Afghanistan's narrow Wakhan Corridor borders Jammu and Kashmir (claimed by both Pakistan and India) and a small portion of China.

◉ Topography

Afghanistan's landscape is divisible into three main geographic areas. These general regions are the northern plains, the central mountain ranges, and the southern lowlands.

The northern plains of Afghanistan border Turkmenistan and Uzbekistan and include elevated plateaus and low hills. Melting snows and local rivers water the region, and local farmers build canals to direct moisture to fields where it is most needed. The fertile soil in the plains supports extensive grasslands on which Afghan herders graze their sheep. Historically, productive farms dotted the valleys that nestled in hills throughout the area. But the landscape bears scars from the conflicts that raged within the country in the late 1900s. Many farming families fled heavy fighting in the northeastern sections of the region, leaving crops and pastureland untended. Fields in these regions were also vulnerable to bombing during the many years of war.

Dominating Afghanistan's topography are the nation's central mountain ranges, which fan out in a wide expanse in the middle of the country. The Paropamisus Mountains, which climb to heights of more than 11,000 feet (3,353 meters) above sea level, rise in western

Afghanistan. As they reach central Afghanistan, these mountains blend into the Koh-i-Baba range, whose peaks rise to almost 17,000 feet (5,182 m). The Koh-i-Baba Mountains form the southwestern portion of the Hindu Kush—the main mountain range in Afghanistan.

The Hindu Kush extends from the middle of Afghanistan, through the Wakhan Corridor to Tajikistan. The range's towering Nowshak Peak is the country's highest summit, rising to 24,551 feet (7,483 m) near the nation's northeastern border with Pakistan. The Safed Koh Range, an offshoot of the Hindu Kush, is shared by Afghanistan and Pakistan. The peaks of this range reach heights of nearly 16,000 feet (4,877 m). Although the steep terrain of the central highlands hinders travel, narrow passes—routes through the ranges—have provided thoroughfares over the centuries for merchants, invaders, and refugees.

KHYBER PASS

The Khyber Pass *(below)* connects Afghanistan with Pakistan through the Safed Koh Range. The pass is more than 30 miles (48 km) long, with its highest point at 3,518 feet (1,072 m) above sea level. As one of the most accessible passes through the mountains of central Asia, the Khyber Pass has been traveled by armies, refugees, and explorers for hundreds of years. Military forts, tombstones, and crumbling ruins offer a glimpse into the Pass's past.

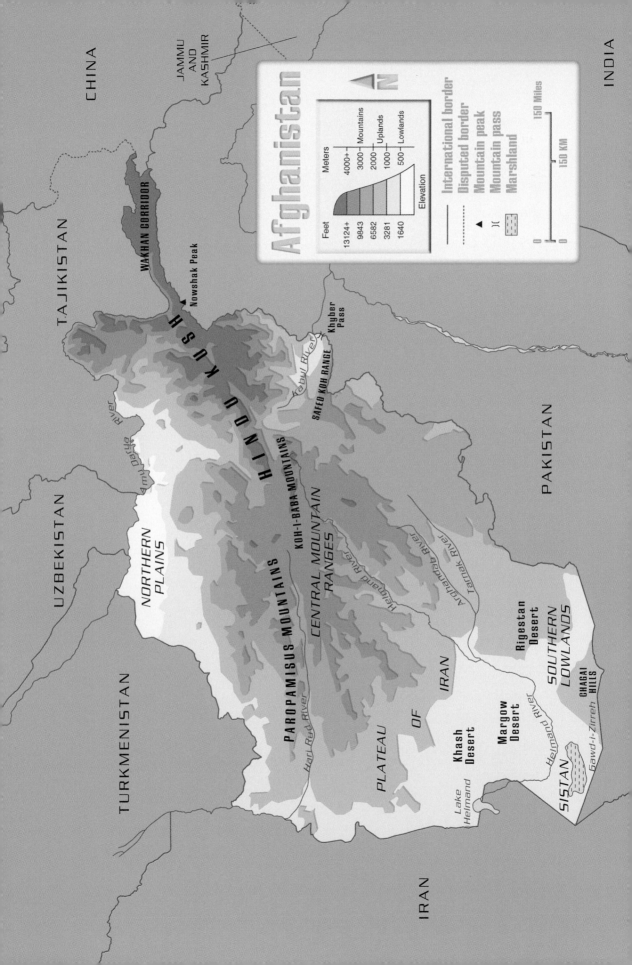

CHINA

JAMMU AND KASHMIR

INDIA

TAJIKISTAN

WAKHAN CORRIDOR

Nowshak Peak

HINDU KUSH

Khyber Pass

SAFED KOH RANGE

Kabul River

UZBEKISTAN

Amu Darya River

NORTHERN PLAINS

PAROPAMISUS MOUNTAINS

KOH-I-BABA MOUNTAINS

CENTRAL MOUNTAIN RANGES

Helmand River

Arghandab River

Tarnak River

PAKISTAN

TURKMENISTAN

Hari Rud River

PLATEAU OF IRAN

Khash Desert

Margow Desert

Rigestan Desert

SOUTHERN LOWLANDS

CHAGAI HILLS

Helmand River

SISTAN

Gawd-i-Zirreh

Lake Helmand

IRAN

Afghanistan

N

Feet	Meters	
13124+	4000+	Mountains
9843	3000	
6582	2000	Uplands
3281	1000	
1640	500	Lowlands

Elevation

International border
Disputed border
Mountain peak
Mountain pass
Marshland

150 Miles

150 KM

This **desert area** in the southwestern part of Afghanistan is home to only a few people. The residents' mud-walled structures are built close to a parched riverbed.

The landscape of the southwestern lowlands rarely rises more than 3,000 feet (914 m) above sea level, except in the far south, where the Chagai Hills mark Afghanistan's border with Pakistan. The Helmand River travels through southern Afghanistan on its way to Iran, but most of the land in the south is desert or semi-desert. The Rigestan Desert covers an extensive corner of southeastern Afghanistan, and the smaller Khash and Margow Deserts lie north of the Helmand River. To the extreme southwest is the Gawd-i-Zirreh, a marshland that occasionally overflows with water in the wet season and merges with Lake Helmand.

These deserts and marshland are part of the Plateau of Iran, a region shared by Afghanistan, Pakistan, and Iran. Less than half of the entire plateau, which covers an area of one million square miles (2.59 million sq. km), lies within Afghanistan.

◉ Rivers

Afghanistan's rivers help provide the nation's farmers with water for irrigation, although some waterways dry up in the summer. The Helmand—the longest river in Afghanistan—originates in the Koh-i-Baba Mountains and flows south for 870 miles (1,400 km) before emptying into Lake Helmand. The lake lies in the Sistan region, a swampy area between Iran and Afghanistan. The Helmand's tributaries, the Arghandab and the Tarnak, provide abundant water for irrigation.

The Kabul River also begins in the Koh-i-Baba, and its 400-mile (644-km) course runs through Afghanistan before flowing north of the Safed Koh's Khyber Pass and into Pakistan. Forming part of Afghanistan's boundary with Tajikistan and Uzbekistan, the Amu Darya River, as well as its tributaries, is fed by the snows of the Hindu Kush. The river eventually winds its way northward to empty into the Aral Sea, which lies in Turkmenistan.

The 700-mile-long (1,127-km) Hari Rud River originates in the Koh-i-Baba Mountains of central Afghanistan and winds through the fertile valley around Herat. The Hari Rud flows on through the

Paropamisus Mountains and turns north to form part of the boundary between Afghanistan and Iran. The river eventually dries up in the deserts of Turkmenistan.

Flora and Fauna

Thick vegetation once grew in Afghanistan's low valleys, but the nation's forest cover decreased dramatically during the latter part of the twentieth century. The country's high mountains are generally treeless and windswept, but some large evergreens, such as cedars, pines, and firs, still exist on the mountainsides. Acacia, walnut, and oak trees survive on the lower slopes. Wildflowers such as wild roses and honeysuckle thrive in the mountains and grasslands of the north. Date palms survive in the south, where scrub vegetation predominates. Herbs of the daisy, mint, and carrot families are abundant.

Afghanistan's rugged terrain is also home to a variety of animals. Gazelles, Afghan foxes, and single-humped dromedary camels live in the plains. Two-humped Bactrian camels inhabit mountain areas. The highlands host snow leopards, wolves, foxes, antelope, ibex (wild goats), markhor sheep, Bactrian deer, brown bears, and Asiatic black bears. Snipes, pelicans, cranes, herons, and sandpipers visit Afghanistan and dwell alongside native pigeons, partridges, pheasants, and woodcocks. Many of Afghanistan's animals are in danger. The primary risks to their survival are habitat loss and hunting by humans.

KING OF KABUL ZOO

One of Afghanistan's most famous animals was not a wild creature. Marjan the lion *(below, with zookeeper)* lived in the Kabul Zoo. Mostly blind, undernourished, and weak after living through two decades of war, Marjan came to represent the resilience of the Afghan people. The lion's story inspired people and animal protection societies around the world to send money to the city's dilapidated zoo. In January 2002, soon after help had arrived, Marjan died in his sleep. But with the help of these badly needed funds, the animals of the Kabul Zoo are eating better and living in warmer and more comfortable cages than they have for many years.

The jagged peaks of the Hindu Kush are usually covered with snow for more than half of the year.

Climate

Situated between the wet monsoon zone of India and arid central Asia, Afghanistan has a generally sunny, dry climate. Because the nation is landlocked, no nearby bodies of water exist to moderate its climate, and it endures extremely hot summers and very cold winters.

In the winter, cold air masses from Siberia (a region of Russia) enter Afghanistan from the north, bringing snow and dropping temperatures. The effects of southern Asia's summer monsoons (seasonal, rain-bearing winds) are felt in the warm months, when heavy rains occur in the Hindu Kush. Strong southwestern winds are also a feature of the summer months in western Afghanistan.

Throughout Afghanistan, extremes in temperature are common, and a day that starts out at 40°F (4°C) can reach 100°F (38°C) by noon. In the northern plains, temperatures average about 38°F (3°C) in January (the coldest month) and 90°F (32°C) in July (the hottest month). Summer temperatures are occasionally much warmer, and the fertile valleys have recorded highs of 120°F (49°C). Annual precipitation in the plains averages only about 7 inches (18 centimeters), half of which falls as snow.

Temperatures in the central highlands reach about 25°F (–4°C) in

> "No place in the world is known to have such a pleasing climate as Kabul."
>
> —from the *Baburnama*, memoirs written by the ruler Babur in the sixteenth century

January and about 75°F (24°C) in July. The country's wettest region, the highlands receive heavy snow, which remains on the highest mountains throughout the year. Lower elevations get about 15 inches (38 cm) of rain annually.

The southwestern lowlands are mainly desert, although the Helmand River waters some areas. The region's temperatures average about 35°F (2°C) in January and about 85°F (29°C) in July. Precipitation in this dry region can be as little as 1 inch (2.5 cm) annually, but some years bring levels of 8 inches (20 cm) or more.

◉ Cities

Afghanistan is a largely rural nation, but it does have several cities of cultural, economic, and political significance. The country's capital city, Kabul, lies along the banks of the Kabul River west of the Koh-i-Baba Mountains. In ancient times, Kabul was a main stop for the trade caravans that streamed through the region from China, and the city eventually became the largest and most important urban center in Afghanistan. Inhabited for more than two thousand years, the city did not become the capital of Afghanistan until 1776. By the early 2000s, the city's population was estimated at more than two million, but a precise figure is difficult to determine because of the large numbers of returning refugees after the fall of the Taliban government in 2001.

Rolling mountains and fertile farmland surround the Afghan capital, Kabul.

Kabul has undergone great change in recent years. Houses in older neighborhoods still have thick walls of mud bricks and roofs of metal. Newer sections of the capital once boasted wide, tree-lined avenues where modern business, government offices, and university buildings were located. In the wake of two decades of conflict, much of Kabul lies in rubble. However, it remains one of Afghanistan's main transportation hubs for export products, which include carpets and dried fruits. The city also has factories that produce plastics, textiles, furniture, and wine.

Qandahar (estimated population 339,000) was founded in the 300s B.C. by invaders from Greece. Present-day Qandahar is the second largest city in Afghanistan and the commercial center of the nation. Lying in a fertile plain in southern Afghanistan, the city is the head-quarters of several industrial projects that use the region's agricultural products as raw materials. Fruit and canning factories operate here, and a textile mill weaves locally grown cotton into cloth.

Herat (estimated population 167,000) was once a depot for silks and gems from India, China, and the Arabian Peninsula. Since its founding in the third century B.C., the city has been invaded many times. Muslim armies took Herat in the seventh century A.D., and the

After the fall of the Taliban, ruined buildings in this busy section of Kabul serve as constant reminders of the city's turbulent past.

Street vendors sell spices and other foods at a Mazar-e-Sharif market.

Mongol conqueror Timur made the city his capital in 1381, transforming it into a center of Islamic art and learning. Residents of modern Herat produce rugs and export fruits.

Mazar-e-Sharif is northern Afghanistan's main urban area, with an estimated population of more than 200,000. The focus of commercial activity in the region, Mazar-e-Sharif is also an important place of Islamic pilgrimage. The city's fifteenth-century mosque (Islamic place of prayer) is believed to hold the tomb of Ali, one of Islam's most important religious leaders.

Visit vgsbooks.com for links to websites where you can find photos and information on Afghanistan's cities and landscapes, up-to-date population figures, current weather conditions, and news about efforts to help the animals of the Kabul Zoo.

HISTORY AND GOVERNMENT

Afghanistan's location at a historical crossroads has led to a steady movement of people through the region. For millennia, peaceful settlers, conquering armies, and adventurous travelers from Asia and beyond have crossed paths on Afghanistan's ancient soil. Archaeological evidence shows that the earliest settlements in the area were founded in about 6000 B.C. Local peoples started out as nomadic herders and eventually developed permanent farming communities. By about 1500 B.C., some of these scattered villages had developed into small urban centers.

◉ Early Invasions

In about 550 B.C., the region that would become Afghanistan came under the authority of the Achaemenids, a dynasty, or family of rulers, from Persia (modern Iran). The Achaemenids conquered the local populations, who resisted fiercely. Persian troops stationed throughout the Hindu Kush controlled the area.

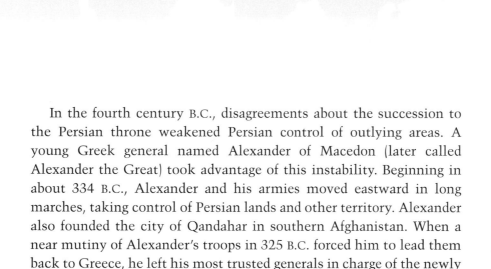

In the fourth century B.C., disagreements about the succession to the Persian throne weakened Persian control of outlying areas. A young Greek general named Alexander of Macedon (later called Alexander the Great) took advantage of this instability. Beginning in about 334 B.C., Alexander and his armies moved eastward in long marches, taking control of Persian lands and other territory. Alexander also founded the city of Qandahar in southern Afghanistan. When a near mutiny of Alexander's troops in 325 B.C. forced him to lead them back to Greece, he left his most trusted generals in charge of the newly conquered areas.

Seleucids, Bactrians, and Parthians

Alexander died two years later, and his generals divided his realm among themselves. The Greek general Seleucus took control of the Persian Empire's lands, including a northern region called Bactria, and founded the Seleucid dynasty. Large numbers of Greek colonists moved to the Hindu Kush, and Greek culture flourished in the area.

Bactria rebelled against Seleucid control in about 250 B.C. The Greek-influenced Bactrians established a strong state that eventually stretched west into Persia, east into India, and south to the Arabian Sea. The Greco-Bactrian Kingdom lasted for about 150 years, until the Parthians from central Asia took over the Persian Empire and gained control of northern and western Afghanistan.

Other powers also competed for the region. The Saka, another central Asian group, controlled southwestern Afghanistan, and the Mauryan dynasty in eastern India extended west to Afghanistan. Mauryan rulers introduced the Bactrians to Buddhism, a religion founded by the Indian philosopher and monk Siddhartha Gautama (Buddha).

○ The Kushan Empire and New Invaders

Afghanistan changed hands again when the Kushan, a powerful group that originated in China, invaded the region around A.D. 50. The Kushan defeated the Parthians and the Saka, united Bactria with Sogdiana (a region to the north), and extended their rule over Kashmir and the Kabul River Valley.

The greatest of the Kushan rulers was Kaniska, who ruled from about A.D. 78 to 103. The Kushan practiced Buddhism, and Kaniska and other leaders fostered the religion in Afghanistan. Buddhist philosophy and art mingled with the earlier Greek influences. Kaniska also supported the arts and strengthened commercial ties along the trade routes that ran through Afghanistan.

By about the 200s, the Kushan Empire had split into small independent kingdoms that became prey first to conquerors from Persia and later from eastern India. New invaders appeared in the early eighth century, when armies from the Arabian Peninsula arrived in Afghanistan. These troops were

A PROFITABLE PATH

The narrow strip of land in northeastern Afghanistan known as the Wakhan Corridor was once part of the Silk Road, a trade route that passed from China through central and southwestern Asia to Europe. The Silk Road was an important economic thoroughfare between the first and fourteenth centuries A.D., and Afghanistan's position along this heavily traveled highway of commerce allowed Kushan merchants to trade widely. The Kushan also served as brokers in commercial exchanges between the Roman Empire and India.

Mongol ruler Genghis Khan leads his troops into battle. Khan used his strong military skills to amass a large empire in eastern and central Asia.

followers of Islam, a religion that had been founded by the prophet Muhammad in about 610. The rulers of the expanding Islamic realm added Afghanistan to their holdings and gradually converted their new subjects to Islam. Throughout the region, semi-independent dynasties rose and fell, and control of Afghanistan rapidly changed hands.

By the end of the tenth century, the Islamic Ghaznavid dynasty had established itself in Ghazni, a city southwest of Kabul. The Ghaznavid ruler Mahmud Khan led annual expeditions into India to convert local populations to Islam and to seize treasures for the kingdom. After Mahmud's death in 1030, the region came under attack by various groups. By 1186, under the leadership of Muhammad of Ghur, Islamic troops of the Ghurid dynasty from northwestern Afghanistan had completely overthrown the Ghaznavids. The Ghurids ruled for less than a century before their control began to falter under sweeping attacks by the central Asian forces of Mongol warrior Genghis Khan.

Mongols

In 1220 the Mongols invaded Afghanistan, plundered its cities, and massacred its people. Genghis Khan died in 1227, and his descendants continued to raid the region. But the vast Mongol Empire, stretching from eastern China to the Caspian Sea in the west, was fragmented. In about 1380, a new conqueror, Timur (also known as Tamerlane), seized northern Afghanistan.

Tamerlane is actually a variation on Timur Lenk, which means "Timur the Lame" in Persian. He earned this nickname after an injury left him with only limited use of one side of his body. Historians disagree over which side was affected and how the injury occurred.

A descendant of Genghis Khan, Timur conquered northern Afghanistan in about 1380. By the end of the fourteenth century, Timur's empire stretched from India to Turkey. Timur died in 1405, and his successors established the Timurid dynasty in Herat. Islam had taken a firm hold in the region by this time, replacing Buddhism as the primary religion. Timurid rulers supported Islamic culture and developed their capital city into a center of art and learning. Commerce and culture thrived until the early sixteenth century, when Zahir-ud-Din Muhammad invaded Afghanistan. Called Babur by his followers, this Mongol conqueror shared the same ancestry as Timur. Babur took Kabul in 1504 and invaded Delhi, India, in 1526, laying the foundations of the Moghul Empire.

Struggle and Unity

With the center of the Moghul Empire far away in Delhi, Afghanistan became easy prey for invaders. For two centuries, the Moghuls, the Safavids from Persia, and the Uzbek from present-day Uzbekistan competed for the region. By the mid-1700s, western Afghanistan had fallen under Persian rule. The Uzbek controlled northern Afghanistan, and eastern Afghanistan remained a remote territory of the Moghul Empire.

Western Afghans soon overthrew the Persians under the leadership of an Afghan general named Mirwais Khan. The Persians, however, regained parts of Afghanistan under their king Nader Shah. When a member of Nader Shah's guard assassinated the ruler in 1747, Afghan leaders again struggled for independence.

One of the most able Afghan fighters was Ahmad Khan, a member of the Abdali Pashtuns. The Abdali were a subgroup of the Pashtuns (also called Pakhtuns or Pathans), the largest of Afghanistan's many distinct ethnic groups. The son of an important Abdali leader, Ahmad had a reputation as a skilled commander and horseman. After Nader Shah's assassination, Ahmad sought to unite Afghan peoples against further occupation. He and other Pashtuns in his clan met to select a leader. Ahmad was chosen as shah (king) in 1747. Ahmad Shah became known as Durr-i-Durran (pearl of pearls), or Ahmad Shah Durrani, and thereafter the Abdali Pashtuns were called the Durrani Pashtuns.

Ahmad Shah's Reign

Ahmad Shah spent much of his twenty-six-year reign subduing new territories, maintaining control over them, and suppressing rebellions. When opposition threatened Ahmad's kingdom, he dealt with it harshly. In northwestern India, the Sikh Kingdom—made up of people who followed the Sikh religion—fought for control of Punjab. Ahmad returned to the region again and again to subdue the Sikhs, and his armies attacked the Sikh holy city of Amritsar, killing thousands and invading places of worship.

Ahmad's armies also marched north of the Hindu Kush to conquer the Tajik, Uzbek, Turkoman, and Hazara clans. His troops pressed toward India, capturing Sind, Punjab, and Kashmir, and plundering and destroying the Indian cities of Lahore and Delhi.

Ahmad was an aggressive military commander and an innovative leader. He ruled his fellow Pashtuns with the help of a council, whose advice he sought on important issues. Through group decision making and by fighting together to gain or hold territory, Afghans came to feel like part of a unified nation for the first time.

Unstable Monarchy

After Ahmad died in 1773, his son Timur Shah succeeded him. Timur did not involve Pashtun leaders in governing as much as his father had, and many Pashtun subgroups rebelled. Moreover, when Timur died in 1793 without declaring an heir, all of his sons—who numbered more than twenty—claimed to be his successor. Eventually Timur's

Ahmad Shah's tomb was built in Qandahar, the city that served as the capital of his empire.

fifth son, Zaman, became shah. But the regime was unstable. Rebellions and coups occurred often as Timur's sons competed for control.

In 1826 a leader named Dost Mohammad Khan took over Kabul. In 1835 he proclaimed himself emir (ruler). Although Dost Mohammad was able to bring most of Afghanistan under his control, two foreign powers—Russia and Britain—challenged his realm. The British were extending their rule over most of the Indian subcontinent (a region in southern Asia that includes modern-day India, Pakistan, and Bangladesh). As the British advanced north and west into India, the Russians moved south to broaden their influence over central Asia. Afghanistan found itself caught between two world powers.

First and Second Anglo-Afghan Wars

After unsuccessful meetings with British officials, who failed to gain Afghanistan's support, Dost Mohammad permitted Russia to station a diplomat in Kabul. Britain felt that Russia's presence threatened British holdings in India and demanded that Dost Mohammad remove the Russian representative. The emir refused, and in March 1838, British and Indian armies invaded Afghanistan.

The First Anglo-Afghan War began a century of intermittent fighting, during which Britain and Russia attempted to conquer or weaken smaller kingdoms that stood in the way of their expansion. The British met with little resistance in Afghanistan, conquering Qandahar in April 1839 and Ghazni in July. Kabul fell in August. The British installed Shah Shoja—one of Timur's sons—as king. Dost Mohammad went into exile in India.

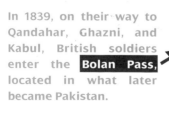

In 1839, on their way to Qandahar, Ghazni, and Kabul, British soldiers enter the **Bolan Pass,** located in what later became Pakistan.

JOURNEY TO JALALABAD

The winter retreat from Kabul, in January 1842, was extremely costly for the British and marked the end of the First Anglo-Afghan War. Traveling through passes choked with snow, and suffering frequent attacks by local warriors, the British lost soldiers all along the route. Of the more than sixteen thousand people who set out on the journey, the army surgeon, Dr. Brydon (*left*), is often listed as the only survivor. However, many historians suggest that others probably survived as hostages and prisoners.

In late 1841, Muhammad Akbar Khan, a son of Dost Mohammad, led a revolt against Shah Shoja. British troops in Afghanistan retreated to Jalalabad early the next year. Shah Shoja was assassinated, and Dost Mohammad regained the throne in 1843.

Dost Mohammad died in 1863, and his potential successors vied for power. His son Shir Ali Khan attained the throne in 1868. In 1878 Russia forced the new king to allow a Russian diplomatic mission in Kabul. This move angered Britain, which demanded that Shir Ali also accept a British mission. Shir Ali refused to permit yet another foreign presence in his nation. In November 1878, the British-Indian army again invaded Afghanistan, launching the Second Anglo-Afghan War.

Shir Ali turned to Russia for help but received none. He died a few months later, and in October 1879, Afghan forces retreated from Kabul. The British quickly captured the city, and in 1880 they placed Abdor Rahman Khan, grandson of Dost Mohammad, on the Afghan throne.

Abdor Rahman modernized the army and reformed the nation's finances. He suppressed crime and curbed local revolts. Not all of his endeavors were positive. In 1893 Abdor Rahman accepted a new eastern boundary proposed by Britain's Sir Mortimer Durand. Called the Durand Line, the division ignored ethnic and geographic considerations. But Abdor Rahman's overall success as Afghanistan's leader was illustrated by the ease with which his son Habibollah Khan succeeded him in 1901. Habibollah carried on many of his father's policies, including the establishment of regional governments and a permanent army.

Early Twentieth Century

Despite Afghanistan's strides toward strong nationhood, outsiders continued to involve themselves in the nation's affairs. In 1907, for example, Britain and Russia signed the Anglo-Russian Convention. This agreement stated that neither Britain nor Russia intended to occupy Afghanistan. Habibollah refused to sign this treaty because he had not participated in negotiating it. Nevertheless, the Russians and the British declared the document to be valid.

During World War I (1914–1918), Habibollah cooperated with the Anglo-Russian Convention by remaining neutral in the conflict. But after he was assassinated in 1919, his successor, Amanollah Khan, declared war on Britain in order to break free from British intervention. The Third Anglo-Afghan War lasted for six weeks and resulted in a new treaty giving Afghanistan free rein in its foreign affairs. The document also ended British financial support.

Amanollah enacted a constitution in 1923 and introduced measures such as education programs for women. In 1929 Afghans who disagreed with Amanollah's modernizing reforms attempted to overthrow him. The rebellion was put down, but Amanollah was forced to yield the throne to Muhammad Nader Khan, a former diplomatic minister. Nader Khan instituted economic reforms and made some progress in uniting the often warring Afghan ethnic groups, but his term ended abruptly when a family enemy assassinated him in 1933.

One of Zahir Shah's efforts to modernize was the Helmand Valley Project. This plan used the irrigation and hydroelectric potential of the Helmand River to open up new farmland in the southwest and to provide hydropower.

The new king, Mohammad Zahir Shah, ascended the throne in November 1933 at the age of nineteen. He took power smoothly, with the backing of three powerful uncles. Zahir Shah spent the first two decades of his forty-year reign under their strong influence.

Zahir Shah's government tried to secure Afghanistan's independent status. Afghanistan joined the League of Nations, an international organization, in 1934 and established ties with other Islamic nations such as Turkey and Iran. During World War II (1939–1945), Zahir Shah kept Afghanistan

During the first decades of his reign, **Zahir Shah** helped establish good relations between his country and the United States and other Western nations.

neutral. He focused his attention on improving his country by expanding economic markets and adopting new technologies.

Daud Khan

Changes also occurred within the royal family. The next generation of leadership sought greater independence and a more modern outlook.

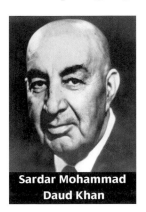

Sardar Mohammad Daud Khan

Sardar Mohammad Daud Khan, one of the king's first cousins, became prime minister in 1953 and took significant steps to modernize Afghanistan. He ordered women not to wear the traditional Islamic veil—a move that angered many members of the Afghan clergy—and accepted foreign loans from both the Soviet Union (a nation made up of republics including Russia) and the United States.

Daud also supported the delicate issue of Pashtunistan, a proposed independent state for Pashtuns in Pakistan. If achieved, the new state would have strong ties with Pashtuns in Afghanistan.

Pakistan's president, Ayub Khan, opposed Pashtunistan. Pakistan and Afghanistan broke diplomatic relations in 1961 over this issue and closed their borders to one another's commerce. This loss of trade seriously damaged Afghanistan's economy.

In 1963, as Prime Minister Daud's policies led to his plummeting popularity, the king removed him from office and adopted a new constitution that established a constitutional monarchy. This change meant a more open form of government in which the king and an elected legislature, or parliament, would jointly rule the nation. Elections for parliament were held in September 1965. Among the new political parties that won several seats was the People's Democratic Party of Afghanistan (PDPA). This organization supported Socialism and Communism, the political theories on which the Soviet Union was based.

The new government soon faced trouble. Taking advantage of the more open system, many newspapers began to publish articles that criticized the regime's control of political affairs. University students and faculty in Kabul demonstrated against government policies. In addition to social unrest, drought threatened the country's economy.

Sensing the government's instability, Daud led a coup in 1973 to depose the king, who was out of the country at the time. Embracing Socialism and Communism in order to gain the PDPA's support, Daud declared Afghanistan to be a republic (a system of government without a monarch). The king remained in exile.

The 1970s

Daud introduced social and economic reforms, along with a new constitution. He eventually began moving away from the PDPA's ideals and its leaders. He also reduced Afghanistan's financial dependence on both the Soviet Union and the United States by forming alliances with Islamic countries. All of these actions weakened Daud's popular support.

The PDPA had troubles of its own, as friction between two of its prominent members, Babrak Karmal and Nur Mohammad Taraki, split the group into two factions. Karmal headed the Parcham group, and Taraki led the Khalq wing of the party. But the factions shared a dislike for Daud, and they reunited in 1977 to plan a coup against him. They assassinated Daud and established the Democratic Republic of Afghanistan on April 27, 1978. Taraki assumed the post of prime minister of the new government, which supported Communism and Socialism. Karmal and the Khalqi leader Hafizullah Amin became deputy prime ministers.

Hafizullah Amin

Having strengthened its Communist ties to the Soviet Union, the new government faced accusations that the Soviet Union controlled the new regime. But PDPA leaders maintained that their policies were based on

Afghan nationalism, social and economic justice, and independence in foreign affairs. The government introduced reforms in land ownership and in women's rights. These moves toward a modernized society angered some Afghans, who felt that they violated Afghan and Islamic traditions. Some Islamic groups began to criticize the nation's interaction with non-Islamic countries. The relationship with the United States, which provided some financial aid to Afghanistan, began to weaken. Meanwhile, violence erupted in eastern Afghanistan in 1978.

Rivalry soon reemerged between the Khalq and Parcham factions of the PDPA. Parcham members, including Karmal, were given diplomatic posts outside the country so that the Khalqis could strengthen their control over the government without interference. In addition, the influence of Hafizullah Amin grew within the administration.

In February 1979, the U.S. ambassador to Afghanistan, Adolph Dubs, was abducted and killed in Kabul. U.S. officials could not determine who had been behind the assassination, but, suspecting Islamic extremists, the United States immediately cut back assistance to Afghanistan. Hoping to foster a strong Socialist government in the nation, the Soviet Union stepped in to offer its support. Amin replaced Taraki as prime minister and sought more Soviet military aid. In 1979 Amin's supporters killed Taraki, who had retained other official

Adolph Dubs

positions. Meanwhile, violence and revolts against the Socialist government continued throughout Afghanistan's rural provinces.

Soviet Takeover and Opposition to Soviet Presence

Concerned by the rural revolts and by the internal political struggles that were weakening the Afghan administration, the Soviet Union sent its troops into Afghanistan in December 1979. Amin and many of his followers died in the fighting that ensued, and the Soviets installed Karmal as prime minister.

Opposition to the Afghan Socialist regime had been mounting during Amin's rule, and anti-Soviet and anti-Karmal factions grew rapidly. By the end of 1980, several groups within Afghanistan had united to resist the Soviet troops and the Soviet-supported Afghan army. Intense fighting erupted between these resistance forces, called the mujahideen, and the Afghan army.

The mujahideen were several well organized groups in Afghanistan

BAND OF FIGHTERS

Many members of the mujahideen *(above)* came from Afghanistan's farming and herding communities. Life among the mujahideen was rough. Fighters lived in remote areas, slept in tents and prepared their meals over outdoor cooking pits. The mujahideen fought with weapons that had been smuggled across the border from Pakistan, and they put up a fierce guerilla-style resistance to the Soviet invasion.

that had emerged in response to political and religious issues. The nonreligious nature of recent regimes offended many Afghans. In addition, government policies aimed at land reform and at the expansion of women's rights threatened the conservative, rural values of most Afghans. Mujahideen fighters sought the creation of an Islamic republic and a return to age-old Islamic and Afghan customs.

Although all mujahideen were Muslim, their approaches to Islamic ideas varied. Traditional ethnic and language bonds also distinguished the various groups of the mujahideen. In the early days of the opposition, these differences frequently became the source of violent internal conflict. But, united under an uneasy truce, the mujahideen joined forces to oppose the Soviets and the Afghan Socialist government.

After 1980 clashes frequently occurred between Soviet-Afghan troops and the mujahideen, who were armed by the United States and other nations. By the late 1980s, approximately thirty thousand Soviet soldiers and about one million Afghans had died in the fighting. An additional three million Afghans—about one-fifth of the population—had moved to refugee camps in Pakistan and Iran. Most mujahideen leaders also left the country, directing their forces from Pakistan. Some hostility grew between these absent leaders and the fighters who stayed in Afghanistan.

Despite growing conflicts among them, the mujahideen controlled nearly all of Afghanistan's mountain regions and the border with Pakistan by the late 1980s. The advanced training, weapons, and support offered to the Afghan government by the Soviet Union were not enough to challenge the rebels' control in the countryside.

⊙ Soviet Withdrawal

In 1985 Prime Minister Karmal tried to boost popular support for his Soviet-backed regime. Rather than appointing more Communists to governmental positions, he chose leaders of national ethnic groups. Meanwhile, the United Nations (UN) sponsored peace talks in Geneva, Switzerland, between U.S. and Soviet negotiators and between representatives of Afghanistan and Pakistan. Pakistan's involvement stemmed from its position as the temporary home of thousands of Afghan refugees and the channel through which the mujahideen received aid and operated the resistance. Since the United States and the Soviet Union provided most of the weaponry used in the conflict, their participation was also essential.

In May 1986, perhaps because of the poor response to Karmal's attempt to gain popular support, the Soviet Union installed a new prime minister, named Najibullah. He, too, made efforts to win approval among the common people. But like Karmal, he had little success.

Meanwhile, UN peace efforts continued, resulting in the withdrawal of the Soviet soldiers. Troop pullouts began in mid-1988 and ended in 1989. The mujahideen, who had rejected the UN proposal because they were not asked to participate in the negotiations, continued their attacks on Najibullah's government in Kabul. Frequent shelling reduced the capital to ruins and forced thousands of residents to flee as the region collapsed into civil war.

With the Soviets gone, Najibullah lost what little support he had, and he resigned in 1992. The mujahideen soon advanced into Kabul, which became the scene of intense fighting. The mujahideen chiefs set up a ruling council, headed by Burhanuddin Rabbani. Later in the year, the mujahideen's new government named Rabbani acting president

Soviet forces pull out of Afghanistan in February 1989.

and proclaimed the founding of the Islamic State of Afghanistan.

In March 1993, the mujahideen groups signed a peace agreement with one another. Rabbani would keep his post as president, and Gulbuddin Hekmatyar, the head of a mujahideen group, would become the head of a council of ministers. Each mujahideen group would appoint two representatives to this council.

Rise and Fall of the Taliban

Despite this power-sharing agreement, conflict among the mujahideen continued. Meanwhile, a group of Pashtun Islamic students living in exile in Pakistan had organized a new faction called the Taliban. A fundamentalist Islamic group, the Taliban wanted to establish a society founded on what they saw as the purest interpretation of Islam, governed by an Islamic leadership that would strictly enforce rigid rules for behavior. Many mujahideen joined the Taliban, attracted by the students' strong commitment to Islam. These mujahideen brought their fighting skills to the group and provided the Taliban with weapons.

Led by a cleric named Mullah Mohammed Omar, Taliban fighters rapidly advanced through eastern Afghanistan. They captured Kabul in September 1996. Swiftly implementing their radical version of Islamic law, they tortured and killed former leader Najibullah and his brother, publicly displaying their bodies and calling them murderers and enemies of Islam. Meanwhile, Rabbani and his allies fled the city, and by the end of the year the Taliban controlled most of the country.

While some mujahideen had become loyal to the Taliban, others opposed the faction's rule. The opposition included Ahmad Shah Massoud, one of the mujahideen's most respected leaders. In addition to being a capable fighter, Massoud was a member of Afghanistan's educated minority and had a master's degree in civil engineering.

Taliban opposition leader **Ahmad Shah Massoud** communicates with other mujahideen by radio.

Searching for refuge, these Afghans crossed rough terrain in cold weather after their village was almost completely destroyed by the February 1998 earthquake.

In the summer of 1997, Massoud, Rabbani, and other political and military leaders created the United National and Islamic Front for the Salvation of Afghanistan (UNIFSA), often called the Northern Alliance. While the Taliban was made up primarily of Pashtuns, Northern Alliance members came from a variety of non-Pashtun ethnic groups. Together, the Alliance fought against the new regime's growing repression. The Taliban's policies were extreme, drastically limiting Afghans' freedom and denying them many basic human rights. Afghan women and ethnic minorities suffered especially harsh treatment, and violators of the Taliban's rules were subject to brutal punishment, including torture and public execution.

In October 1997, the Taliban renamed the country the Islamic Emirate of Afghanistan and raised a new flag. Meanwhile, many Afghans remained very unhappy with the strictly fundamentalist regime. The fight against the Taliban continued.

Conditions worsened in 1998 when the nation was hit by massive earthquakes. Striking in February and May, the quakes killed more than nine thousand people and left tens of thousands homeless. As Afghans struggled to rebuild, a new challenge arose. The United States was threatening to use military force against the Afghan government for sheltering the Saudi-born terrorist Osama bin Laden. U.S. officials believed that bin Laden and his organization, al-Qaeda, had played a role in terrorist acts, including a 1993 bombing of the World Trade Center in New York City and 1998 bombings of U.S. embassies in

FRIEND OF THE TALIBAN

Osama bin Laden *(above)* was born in 1957 in Saudi Arabia, where he grew up in a prominent Muslim family. In the 1980s, he traveled to Afghanistan to fight the Soviets with the mujahideen. He returned to Saudi Arabia after the Soviets retreated, but his increasingly radical view of Islam and his anti-government activities eventually resulted in the loss of his Saudi citizenship. Bin Laden returned to Afghanistan in 1996, and from there he operated al-Qaeda, a group that he formed to plan and commit terrorist acts against nations he and his supporters view as enemies of Islam.

Africa. The Taliban refused to comply with mounting pressure to yield bin Laden to international authorities, and the United States responded with bombings targeting suspected terrorist training camps in Afghanistan. Meanwhile, the Taliban continued to extend their control. By the end of 2000, 95 percent of the nation was under Taliban rule, and the United States had imposed economic restrictions on the country for continuing to harbor bin Laden.

In September 2001, Massoud was assassinated. The influential leader's death came as a blow to the mujahideen groups, and many people feared that the resistance movement would crumble without Massoud's guidance. A few days later, on September 11, hijacked airplanes struck the Pentagon in Washington, D.C., and the twin towers of the World Trade Center in New York. With a death toll of close to three thousand people, the events of September 11 were the largest terrorist attacks ever to occur on U.S. soil. Once again, bin Laden and al-Qaeda were believed to be behind the acts. In October 2001, after the Taliban repeated their refusal to hand over bin Laden, U.S. and British airborne forces launched strikes on Afghanistan.

As the U.S. offensive turned into a full-scale war, the Northern Alliance took advantage of foreign support to defeat the Taliban. By the end of November 2001, the Alliance

Emboldened by U.S. support, **Northern Alliance fighters** attacked Taliban troops near Kabul in November 2001.

had taken the cities of Mazar-e-Sharif and Kabul, and many Taliban and al-Qaeda members fled the country or went into hiding.

◉ A New Phase

Hamid Karzai

In December 2001, Afghanistan swore in an interim government to replace the Taliban. Headed by Hamid Karzai, a relative of former king Mohammad Zahir Shah, the new government began reconstructing the nation's services and systems.

The conflict did not end completely with the fall of the Taliban. Renewed fighting between rival warlords for control of provincial areas erupted in the countryside, threatening the country's tenuous hold on stability. In addition, international troops, including U.S. and British forces, stayed on in Afghanistan to continue searching for Taliban and al-Qaeda fighters and to provide security.

In April 2002, Afghans were pleased to welcome Mohammad Zahir Shah back to the country after twenty-nine years of exile in Italy.

Although not in a position of power in the new government, the former king was still a popular figure, particularly among Pashtuns, and he served as a symbol of unity and patriotism for the nation. Afghanistan took yet another step toward rebuilding in June 2002, when Karzai was appointed to serve as the nation's new president. By the end of 2002, Afghanistan was enjoying greater peace and stability than it had known in more than twenty years.

Government

The government that took power in June 2002 was selected by an emergency *loya jirga,* or grand council. The loya jirga is a centuries-old governmental tool in Afghanistan. These councils have been used to adopt constitutions, place new monarchs on the throne, and make other important national decisions. *Shuras,* or local councils, choose electors, who in turn elect delegates to attend the loya jirga. Delegates have traditionally been tribal leaders, representing many of Afghanistan's ethnic groups and religions. The delegates chosen in 2002 also included eleven women.

After the loya jirga took place, selected delegates from the council

During the June 2002 **loya jirga,** a delegate from southern Afghanistan applauds a speech.

went on to determine a structure for the new government. President Karzai, several vice presidents, and a cabinet of ministers make up the executive branch, with a legislative branch composed of a parliament.

As Karzai and other national leaders worked to establish a framework for the new government, the legal system that would emerge in Afghanistan remained uncertain. Some Afghans wish to continue observing a version of Sharia, or Muslim law. Others prefer the more moderate civil and criminal law established in the 1964 constitution. A 2001 United Nations agreement proposing goals and guidelines for Afghanistan's reconstruction stated that the transitional government would "rebuild the domestic justice system in accordance with Islamic principles, international standards, the rule of law and Afghan legal traditions." Achieving this delicate balance between outside pressures and national customs will be a challenge for leaders in all areas of the country's government.

Afghanistan's future is still uncertain, and the nation is still in turmoil. To track current developments in Afghanistan's story, visit vgsbooks.com for links to websites where you can find the most up-to-date news and information.

THE PEOPLE

About 27.8 million people live in Afghanistan. Between the beginning of the Afghan war in 1979 and the reign of the Taliban, more than 3 million Afghans fled to Pakistan and Iran. However, since the Taliban's fall and the return of a tentative peace to Afghanistan, hundreds of thousands of Afghan refugees and emigrants have streamed back into the country. While these returning Afghans have much to offer their recovering nation, the rapid influx of so many people threatens to over-burden the country's limited supplies of food and shelter.

The majority of Afghans reside in rural areas in homes made of sun-dried bricks. Seasonal herders live in goatskin tents. City dwellers—who make up 22 percent of the population—often live in mud dwellings or in concrete structures. During the civil war of the early 1990s, a rising number of urban residents crowded Kabul and other cities. When the Taliban held Kabul, many people fled, but the instal-lation of a new government has drawn many former Kabul residents back, along with newcomers.

web enhanced @ www.vgsbooks.com

Ethnic Groups

Because of Afghanistan's location near historic international trade routes, the nation's people represent a mix of ethnic and language groups. Few of these groups are contained entirely within Afghanistan, because international boundaries cut through many strong ethnic communities. There are around fifty ethnic groups in all, but most Afghans belong to one of two main Indo-European ethnic groups—the Pashtuns and the Tajiks. In the north are the Uzbeks and the Turkomans, who are both Turkic-speaking minorities. Small groups of Hazaras—farmers of central Asian ancestry—and Nuristanis, who live close to the border with Pakistan, also dwell in Afghanistan.

Pashtuns make up about 35 to 38 percent of the population. However, the Pashtuns are further divided into many smaller groups. The Durrani Pashtuns, for example, come from the Abdali clan from which the eighteenth-century leader Ahmad Shah was descended. Some Pashtuns are traditionally nomadic herders whose historical

AN ANCIENT CODE OF HONOR

Pashtun men *(right)* and boys follow a strict code of behavior known as Pashtunwali. This code, which plays a significant role in Pashtun society, is comprised of three main ideals. *Nanawatey* requires Pashtuns to assist all living creatures who seek protection. *Badal* requires Pashtuns to retaliate or seek vengeance for wrongs done to themselves or their family or friends. *Melmastia* requires Pashtuns to offer their hospitality to all guests. This supremely important code of honor dates back to before Islam's arrival in Afghanistan.

routes of migration have been severely disrupted by many years of war. Other subgroups of this Afghan ethnic community work in urban areas or in the countryside as farmers or herders. Although they have established ethnic pockets throughout the nation, Pashtuns generally live in a broad, semicircular area in central Afghanistan. Substantial numbers also live in Pakistan near the Afghan border. Pashtuns speak Pashto, one of the nation's two main languages.

Tajiks, Afghanistan's second largest ethnic group, make up 25 to 30 percent of the population and generally live in the northeast. Many also reside in the west near the city of Herat and in the northwest. Most rural Tajiks are uneducated farmers, but city dwellers tend to be educated and are often employed as tradespeople, artisans, or government workers. They speak dialects of Dari, an Indo-European language related to Farsi, which is spoken in Iran.

Turkomans and Uzbeks live in Afghanistan as well as in Turkmenistan and Uzbekistan. They speak Turkic languages that are not related to the Indo-European family. Together these groups represent less than 15 percent of Afghanistan's population. Most of them are farmers or herders, but some have moved to urban centers, where they can find better schools and higher-paying jobs. Many Uzbeks raise the valuable karakul sheep or breed horses, while Turkoman craftspeople are especially known for their hand-woven carpets.

These young **Hazara girls** live in Kabul, but many other Hazaras live in mountainous areas of the country, where they farm and breed sheep.

Central Afghanistan is home to the Dari-speaking Hazaras. Their mountainous territory in the Hindu Kush is difficult to farm, and many Hazaras have moved to Afghan cities and towns. Most Hazaras are Shiite Muslims, a stricter sect of Islam than the more numerous Sunnis. Of Mongol ancestry, some Hazaras believe that they are descendants of the warrior Genghis Khan.

A small number of Nuristanis, who are mostly farmers and herders, reside in eastern Afghanistan. The Nuristanis were one of the last groups in Afghanistan to begin practicing Islam, converting to the religion around the turn of the twentieth century. Prior to that time, they followed traditional customs including ancestor worship. Some historians once believed that the group included descendants of Alexander the Great's soldiers or of Greek settlers in Afghanistan. This theory has been strongly challenged by modern researchers, but the Nuristanis' many distinct differences from other Afghan ethnic groups—such as their languages, music, dwellings, religious traditions, and physical features—continue to provoke interest in their ancient heritage.

Language

Dari (also called Afghan Farsi or Afghan Persian) and Pashto are the two official languages of Afghanistan. Both part of the Indo-European family of languages, they use an Arabic alphabet and are read from right to left. Both languages are taught in schools. Although Dari is the most widely spoken tongue, the government has historically given preference to Pashto in an effort to increase its usage.

In addition to Dari and Pashto, more than twenty-five other languages and dialects are spoken around the country, and many Afghans can speak more than one language. People in the north, where Uzbek and Turkoman ethnic groups dominate, speak Turkic dialects. They share these languages with residents of neighboring nations such as Uzbekistan and Turkmenistan.

Education

Afghanistan has a long history of education. Works written by Afghan intellectuals and scholars date back hundreds of years. Children's education traditionally rested in the hands of Islamic clerics, who instructed their students in subjects including reading, writing, mathematics, and the study of the Quran (the holy text of Islam). In the late 1860s, Shir Ali Khan introduced educational reforms and opened free public schools. After the Soviet invasion in 1979, the Afghan government—supported financially by the Soviet Union—expanded education further. New laws required all children between the ages of seven and ten to attend school.

In modern Afghanistan, technical, art, business, and medical schools exist for higher education. Kabul University, founded in 1932, offers courses in medicine, science, agriculture, engineering, law, political science, and economics. A university in Jalalabad and a vocational school in the capital opened during the 1960s.

After the disruption of the nation's educational system under the Taliban and during the nation's decades of war, Afghanistan's children are going back to school. School officially reopened on March 23, 2002. About 60,000 teachers and 1.5 million students across the country—boys and girls—showed up for the first day.

However, most of the Afghan population remains uneducated. Years of war damaged school buildings and made supplies difficult to obtain. Education also suffered significantly under Taliban rule. The Taliban forbade most women to work outside the home. This edict crippled the school system, whose teachers were mostly women. In addition, all girls over the age of eight were prohibited from attending school from 1998 until the overthrow of

By the spring of 2002, these **female students and their teacher** were able to return to the classroom, although their school had been severely damaged during the civil war.

the Taliban in 2001. Despite the law, some girls secretly attended makeshift schools in private homes.

As Afghan schools rebuild, literacy is a major concern. In 2000 only an estimated 52 percent of Afghan males and 22 percent of females over the age of fifteen could read or write. But international aid organizations such as the United Nations Educational, Scientific and Cultural Organization (UNESCO) are working to help rebuild schools, train teachers, and print textbooks in Dari, Pashto, Uzbek, and other languages.

◉ Health

Poverty, war, and drought affect health statistics in modern Afghanistan. Among Asian countries, Afghanistan has the highest annual death rate (19 deaths per 1,000 people), the highest annual infant death statistic (154 per 1,000 live births), and the lowest life expectancy (45 years). Afghanistan also has one of the highest rates of pregnancy-related mortality in the world, an estimated average of 50 deaths each day.

Afghan clinics and health professionals tend to cluster in Kabul and other cities, leaving rural residents largely unable to access health care. The combinations of war, large-scale emigration, and the

This Afghan doctor does not work in a clinic. He treats a patient on a street in Charikar, north of Kabul.

Taliban's 1996 prohibition of the employment of women led to a sharp decline in the number of qualified medical personnel, and by 2002, there was only about 1 physician for every 50,000 people. Many clinics had to close their doors. In some areas, international relief agencies provided the sole source of treatment and medicine. Even these organizations struggled to keep operating as their workers risked attack and injury in the midst of the war.

Thousands of Afghan children have been orphaned. Many others are from families that are struggling to survive. Terre des Hommes, an international organization dedicated to the welfare of children, estimates that in the early 2000s more than 30,000 children were working and begging in Kabul to support themselves and their families.

Conditions are still poor following the war's end. Unable to reach medical facilities or, in many cases, to pay for health care, many Afghans continue to suffer from treatable diseases, such as malaria, measles, and tuberculosis. Communicable diseases spread rapidly because of inadequate hygiene and sanitation. Less than one-quarter of the total population has clean drinking water, particularly in rural areas. Among children, diseases that could be prevented by vaccination are the cause of approximately 21 percent of deaths. Measles alone kills about 35,000 children each year.

More than twenty years of war have also left Afghanistan with a large number of injured and disabled residents. Even in peaceful times, land mines are an ongoing hazard. The United Nations estimates that up to ten million unexploded mines remain in Afghanistan. Approximately 10 people are injured or killed by these weapons each day. In 2001 cluster bombs dropped by U.S. aircraft brought a new danger. Each cluster bomb sent out 202 small "bomblets," and unexploded bomblets on the ground can easily be set off by touch. Demining agencies have been working to clear Afghanistan of mines for many years, but the work is dangerous and proceeds slowly.

Drought is yet another challenge to the health of Afghans as water shortages continue to impact farming and to thereby deplete food sources. In 2002 the nation was suffering from a drought of more than four years' duration. War, which has disrupted the agricultural economy, further decreases the food supply and makes malnutrition a major cause of disease and death. Approximately 1 in 10 Afghan children is severely malnourished, and starvation remains a pressing concern as health care professionals and international aid organizations attempt to improve conditions in Afghanistan.

In an effort to make this field safe for planting new crops, a deminer searches for unexploded land mines, a hazard resulting from many years of war in Afghanistan.

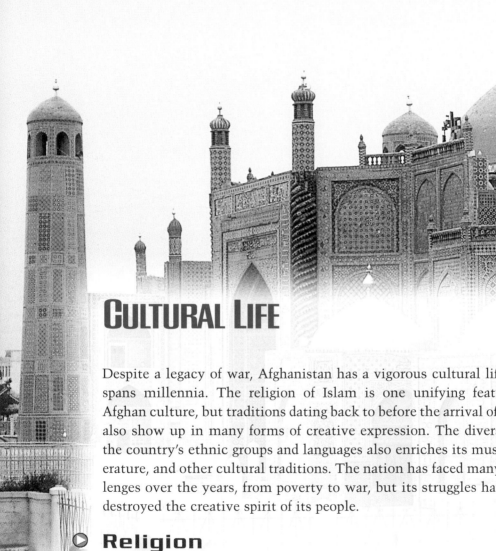

CULTURAL LIFE

Despite a legacy of war, Afghanistan has a vigorous cultural life that spans millennia. The religion of Islam is one unifying feature of Afghan culture, but traditions dating back to before the arrival of Islam also show up in many forms of creative expression. The diversity of the country's ethnic groups and languages also enriches its music, literature, and other cultural traditions. The nation has faced many challenges over the years, from poverty to war, but its struggles have not destroyed the creative spirit of its people.

Religion

Almost all Afghans are Muslims. This common heritage, however, does not mean that they all belong to the same sect of Islam or that they share identical beliefs.

Islam began on the Arabian Peninsula in the seventh century A.D., when the prophet Muhammad began to preach a faith based on submission to one god—Allah—and on the word of Allah as given in the

Quran. Muslim traders, warriors, and leaders spread the religion. They brought it to Afghanistan in about A.D. 700.

Around the same time that Islam arrived in Afghanistan, the faith split into factions. The main subgroups called themselves Sunnis (those who follow the traditional practices of sunna, the example of Muhammad) and Shiites (those who accept the guidelines of Ali, Muhammad's cousin and son-in-law). Sunnis elect their Islamic leaders. Shiites regard Ali as Prophet Muhammad's true successor and support only those religious leaders who are descendants of Muhammad's family. Most Afghan Muslims belong to the Sunni sect, although the Hazara are Shiites.

◉ Holidays and Festivals

With its overwhelming majority of Muslims, most of Afghanistan's holidays and festivals are based on Islamic beliefs and traditions. An important holiday season is the Islamic holy month of Ramadan.

THE FIVE PILLARS OF ISLAM

An important part of each Muslim's life is the observance of five basic tenets of the faith. These principles are known as the Five Pillars of Islam:

Shahada: Declaration of faith. Muslims state that Allah is the only god, and that Muhammad is Allah's prophet.

Salat: Prayer. Muslims pray five times a day.

Zakat: Charity. Muslims donate a portion of their income to the poor.

Sawm: Fasting. Muslims fast during Ramadan, a holy month in the Islamic calendar.

Hajj: Pilgrimage. Muslims try to make a trip to Mecca, Saudia Arabia, once during their lifetime. Mecca is the holiest city of Islam.

Visit vgsbooks.com for links to websites with additional information about Islam.

Ramadan observes the passing of the Quran from Allah to Muhammad. The month is a time for fasting and serious prayer. Most adult Muslims neither eat nor drink from sunup to sundown during this month. During the day, Muslim Afghans may choose to attend special holiday services at mosques. After dark a meal called *iftar* is eaten. Many Muslims break their daylong fast by eating a date, which, according to Islamic tradition, was the way that Muhammad broke his fasts. At the end of Ramadan, Muslims celebrate with the feast of Eid al-Fitr, a three-day holiday of great festivities and rejoicing.

Other important holidays are Mawlid (Muhammad's birthday), Ashura (celebrated by Shiites only in honor of a martyred Shiite leader), and Eid al-Adha (Feast of the Sacrifice). Eid al-Adha's three-day celebration falls during the hajj, the annual pilgrimage to the Islamic holy city of Mecca in Saudi Arabia. Every Muslim must try to make the hajj once during his or her lifetime, and part of the festival is the celebration of the pilgrims' journey.

In March, Afghan Muslims celebrate the Islamic New Year. For many Muslims, this is a time for quiet worship. They may pay visits to mosques or to the grave sites of ancestors. Some people also gather to eat special foods and listen to music. Afghanistan combines this occasion with Farmers' Day, a celebration in honor of the upcoming planting season.

Afghanistan's nonreligious holidays include Labor Day (May 1), Remembrance Day for Martyrs and Disabled (May 4), and Independence Day (August 19). Independence Day, or Jeshen, marks the Third Anglo-Afghan War and the subsequent end of British political influence over Afghanistan. The Taliban outlawed some of these

Young people in Herat celebrate Eid al-Fitr at a street festival.

celebrations as un-Islamic, but they are once again being freely observed under the post-Taliban government.

◉ Literature

Poetry—especially spoken poetry—is Afghanistan's most important literary form. Many of the cultures that flourished in Afghanistan over the years encouraged the writing and memorizing of verse. Poets of the past include Rabia Balkhi, who in the ninth century was the first woman known to compose poetry in Persian (a language closely related to Dari). Other well known poets were Hanzala of Badghis in the ninth century, Abu Shukur of Balkh in the tenth century, Jalal ad-Din ar-Rumi in the thirteenth century, and Khushhal Khan Khatak in the seventeenth century. Many of these poets expressed themes of unattainable love or glorified the warrior spirit in their works.

The tradition continues, and modern Afghan poets produce works in Dari, Pashto, and Turkic. They also enjoy reciting the works of poets from bygone eras. Khalilullah Khalili was a beloved native poet of the twentieth century and has often been referred to as the poet laureate of Afghanistan. Other contemporary authors include Nasrullah Hafez, Mohammad Rahim el-Ham, and A. R. Pazhwak. During the Taliban's reign, when poetry and many other artistic pursuits were banned, some Afghan poets continued to gather secretly with fellow writers to discuss their work. To protect themselves from punishment, they memorized their own poems so that they would not risk being caught carrying copies.

Food and Clothing

Afghans have faced frequent food shortages in recent decades. However, when supplies are plentiful, pilau—rice mixed with meat and vegetables—is served throughout Afghanistan. Saffron, a spice sometimes added during cooking, turns the rice a bright yellow. Pilau is such a common dish that the word has come to mean food in general. *Bolani,* spicy vegetable pies, and *korma,* a vegetable side dish, are other favorites.

PILAU WITH CARROTS AND RAISINS

This popular Afghan dish, called *qabili pilau,* brings together a delicious combination of flavors. Saffron gives the rice a bright yellow color that contrasts nicely with the carrots and raisins.

6 tablespoons vegetable oil

2 medium onions, chopped

1 pound lamb or chicken, cut into bite-sized pieces

1 to 2 cups water

1 teaspoon ground cinnamon

1 teaspoon ground cumin

1 teaspoon ground cardamom

¼ teaspoon saffron (optional)

1 teaspoon salt

2 large carrots, cut into pieces the size of matchsticks

½ cup raisins

salt and black pepper to taste

2½ cups long-grain rice

4 to 5 cups water

1. Heat oil in a large saucepan. Add onion. Sauté until browned.
2. Add meat to pan. Sauté until browned. Add 1 to 2 cups of water (or enough to cover the onion and meat), cinnamon, cumin, cardamom, and saffron (if using), and 1 teaspoon salt. Bring to a boil, then lower heat, and simmer for about one hour, or until meat is tender.
3. Add carrots and raisins. Season with salt and pepper to taste.
4. Preheat oven to 300°F.
5. Place uncooked rice in a large, oven-safe casserole dish with a tightly fitting lid. Top with the meat mixture and add 4 to 5 cups water (or enough to cover the meat and rice by about ½ inch). Bring to a boil. Lower heat, cover, and simmer for 10 to 12 minutes, or until the rice is tender and the water has been absorbed.
6. Place covered casserole dish in oven and bake for 45 minutes. Serve in a large dish or platter, with extra raisins and carrots on top.

Serves 4.

Afghan bread is usually made of whole wheat flour, although other grains, such as barley, corn, or millet, may also be used. Cooks bake some breads in ovens built into the ground and form other loaves into flat rounds that are fried on griddles. Afghans often eat fresh fruit after a meal, and they also enjoy a variety of rich sweets. *Jelabi* (deep-fried pieces of wheat bread coated with syrup) and *gur* (molasses) are common desserts.

Both black and green teas accompany meals and are often spiced with cardamom. Some Afghans dunk a lump of sugar in tea before eating the soaked sugar for refreshment, or they may drink the tea through a sugar cube held between their teeth.

Clothing in Afghanistan, for both men and women, is generally loose-fitting and flowing. Cotton shirts and baggy trousers are common garb, and women also dress in long skirts made of brightly dyed cloth. Heavy coats are worn when the weather turns cold in November.

Men often wear turbans—long pieces of cloth wrapped around the head—or turbanlike caps. The turbans may be tied in distinctive ways to indicate ethnic affiliation. For women, the traditional head covering is a shawl, which they may pull across their faces in the presence of strangers. In keeping with Islamic ideals of modesty, many Afghan women wear an overgarment called a *burqa*, or chador, a long, hooded robe that reveals only the wearer's eyes. The wearing of the burqa is no longer strictly enforced, as it was during the Taliban's reign, but it is still commonly worn.

These Afghan women wear burqas. Many Muslims in Afghanistan believe that women protect their honor and dignity by covering their faces and bodies.

Music, Dance, and Recreation

Although musical styles vary among Afghanistan's ethnic groups and from region to region, traditional music and dance play a major role in nearly every Afghan's cultural life. In a population that generally cannot read or write, music and dance preserve historical and ethnic ties.

Ballads, dances, and stories are performed throughout Afghanistan, accompanied by traditional instruments. Stringed instruments such as the *tar*, the *rubab*, and the *tamboura*, are important to Afghan music. Drums, such as the *dhol* and *daira*, and wind instruments, including the *toula* and *surnay*, are also commonly used.

Many Afghan songs retell the popular legend of Leyli and Majnun. The young couple is deeply in love, but Leyli's father forbids their marriage. Driven mad by his despair, Majnun wanders the desert composing and singing love poetry for Leyli. Finally, consumed by their doomed love, Leyli and Majnun die of sorrow. The story of Leyli and Majnun has also been told in operas, poems, and movies.

Modern artists also contribute to Afghanistan's musical heritage. They often combine traditional instruments and forms with new styles. Radio Afghanistan (formerly Radio Kabul) has been a major force in Afghanistan's musical life since the station's founding in 1925. This national station broadcasts news, radio dramas, folk music, and new popular music. For many Afghans, the radio station was a common bond that bridged ethnic and regional differences. In the 1970s, Radio Afghanistan helped launch many musicians to fame, such as the singers Ahmad Zahir and Farida Mahwash. Contemporary artists, such as Farhad Darya and Ahmad Wali, command large followings in Afghanistan and among Afghan emigrants around the world. Although music was banned during the rule of the Taliban, which viewed it as un-Islamic, Afghan musicians are once again practicing their art in the post-Taliban nation. Afghans, with the aid of international organizations, are also working to reconstruct their national media under the new government.

Dance is also a beloved cultural expression, and the *attan* is considered Afghanistan's national dance. This Pashtun war dance is performed at weddings and other special occasions. Dancers form a large circle and quicken their movements as the tempo of the music increases.

Beyond music, recreation in Afghanistan ranges from picnicking to

These horsemen in Mazar-e-Sharif show off their riding skills as they get ready for **a game of buzkashi.**

playing a traditional, spirited game known as *buzkashi*. In this ancient Afghan sport, dozens of riders on horseback try to pick up the headless carcass of a calf or goat and carry it to a goal. Buzkashi is most often played in northern Afghanistan, and participants often display high-quality horsemanship. Wrestling is also a popular sport. Game rules allow players to grab opponents' arms and clothing but never their legs. At the end of a match, wrestlers may be wearing little more than shreds of fabric.

Sports from Europe and the Americas, including soccer, field hockey, and golf, were introduced in Afghanistan in the mid-twentieth century. But Olympic sports in which Afghans have competed, such as wrestling and weight lifting, are related to traditional athletic pursuits.

Visual Arts

Over the years, Afghanistan has experienced influxes of culture from central, eastern, and southwestern Asia, along with India and the Mediterranean. The area has also been home to Buddhism, Islam, and other ancient beliefs. As a result, visual arts in Afghanistan have a long and colorful history, with both native and foreign origins. Archaeological digs in Afghanistan have turned up a host of ancient treasures. Painted pottery dating back to around 2500 B.C. has been found near Qandahar, and Greek coins discovered north of the Hindu Kush may have been carried by Alexander the Great's soldiers in the 300s B.C.

When Buddhism flourished under the reign of the Kushans (about

A.D. 50 to A.D. 250), Greek and Roman traditions mingled with Buddhism. The result was Greco-Buddhist sculpture and painting with Buddhist subjects—most often Buddha himself—depicted in a European style.

Although sculpture has a longer history than painting in Afghanistan, the nation boasts masters including the fifteenth century miniaturist Behzad of Herat. His small, intricately detailed paintings offer a glimpse of daily life during the Timurid period. The School of Fine Arts opened in Kabul in the 1920s, and Ustad Mashal and Ustad Mohammad Aziz were two major painters of the twentieth century. Although many modern Afghan artists, such as Amanullah Haidarzad, have left Afghanistan because of war and political turmoil, their homeland and traditions continue to influence their work.

Much of Afghanistan's art has been lost. The national museum in Kabul once housed artifacts and art spanning more than twelve centuries. However, the museum was nearly destroyed by war, and its treasures were looted and vandalized. When the Taliban was in power, government officials ruled that many forms of art were un-Islamic. For example, the Buddhas of Bamian, classic pieces of Greco-Buddhist art, once stood near a town northwest of Kabul. Carved from sandstone cliffs, the tallest of these statues was 174 feet (53 m) high, dating from the fifth century A.D., and the oldest statue dated back to the third century A.D. Deemed sacrilegious and un-Islamic by Taliban officials,

This Buddha statue at Bamian stood for more than 1,500 years. In 2001 it was destroyed by the Taliban.

the statues were destroyed in March 2001. Many of Afghanistan's other treasures shared the Buddhas' fate.

In the aftermath of the conflicts of the early 2000s, Afghan and international organizations are striving to restore the nation's art. Contemporary Afghan artists also continue to produce new works. Handicrafts and other traditional arts also help to preserve the country's cultural heritage. Crafts-people, particularly in rural areas, produce rugs, leather goods, and gold and silver jewelry using age-old techniques.

A newer medium for Afghan artists is film. Afghan cinema has existed since the 1940s and has produced films such as *Rozhai Dushwar (Difficult Days)* and *Garatgaran (Thieves).* In 2002 the first films to be shown since the rise of the Taliban were screened in Mazar-e-Sharif. *Grobat* and *Chopandaz,* by director Siddiq Obadi, give viewers a glimpse of Afghan culture and history.

PAINTINGS IN PERIL

When the Taliban was in power, it banned all artworks portraying people and animals. To protect finished paintings from being destroyed, an Afghan doctor and part-time artist named Mohammad Yousof Asefi carefully covered dozens of the forbidden images with layers of watercolor. After the Taliban's fall, Asefi's watercolor coats were carefully removed, and the restored paintings were displayed in the National Gallery in Kabul.

THE ECONOMY

Afghanistan is one of the world's least economically developed nations. War, floods, drought, and earthquakes have disrupted the Afghan economy and slowed progress over many years. In 2002 the Asian Development Bank estimated that the country's annual income per capita was only $200. Unemployment is extremely high, and the value of the afghani, Afghanistan's national currency, has dropped drastically in recent years.

After the Taliban's rule and the conflict that followed, Afghanistan's government has worked with international funds to rebuild the nation's economy. Programs have been implemented to create jobs, boost exports, modernize agriculture and industry, and repair the country's infrastructure. In October 2002, Afghanistan's central bank issued new currency. Afghans were able to trade in one thousand old afghanis for one new afghani. The goal was to restore the currency's value. If successful, all of these developments will help prepare Afghanistan for the future.

Agriculture

Afghanistan remains a primarily rural society, with farming and raising livestock as the chief livelihoods. Only about 12 percent of the land is suitable for crops, and less than half of that is regularly cultivated. Farmers use the remaining acreage as pastureland. Agriculture is estimated to employ more than three-quarters of the nation's workers, while it makes up less than half of Afghanistan's gross national product, or GNP (the total amount of goods and services produced within a nation in a year).

Wheat has traditionally been Afghanistan's main crop and most important food. Afghan farms harvested an estimated 2.5 million tons (2.3 million metric tons) of wheat annually in the 1990s, but severe drought in the late 1990s and early 2000s crippled production. Other major crops are vegetables, rice, barley, and cotton. Grapes and other fruit remain important products for export.

Because of the nation's largely mountainous and dry terrain, most

Wheat is one of Afghanistan's most important crops.

crops are grown in the fertile plains and valleys near sources of water or with the help of irrigation. Government projects in the southwest use the Helmand River for irrigation. Some desert areas have been transformed into productive farmland. However, the nation's instability has hampered the projects' success, and the amount of irrigated land in Afghanistan is estimated to have dropped by more than one-half since 1996.

In addition to crops, livestock are also central to rural communities. Farmers raise animals for their meat, milk, and wool. Cattle and donkeys perform valuable work pulling equipment and loads on farms. Sheep and goats are raised in the greatest numbers. In northern Afghanistan, the karakul sheep is the most valuable breed, and the fur of this animal is highly prized. The export of karakul pelts has been one of the few enterprises in Afghanistan to earn substantial foreign income. However, criticism of the industry by animal rights groups who object to the way the skins are obtained may limit future trade in the pelts.

In the spring of 2002, Afghan farmers, already struggling against drought, faced a new challenge as millions of locusts swarmed over the land. These grasshopper-like insects can consume their own weight in food each day. The United Nations implemented programs to control the insects' spread, which could have destroyed millions of dollars worth of much needed wheat.

Many aspects of Afghanistan's agricultural sector have been eroded by war and turmoil. Many farmers and herders have fled the country, and bombing has destroyed farms and crops. The conflicts have also disrupted food supply to cities, and food shortages occurred throughout the 1990s. The country was forced to import large shipments of staples, such as wheat, and prices rose sharply. Supplies became even scarcer during the conflict of 2001 and 2002, and international aid organizations worked hard to bring enough food into the country to prevent mass starvation. To help Afghanistan's farmers get back on their feet, the Afghan interim government and international groups provided more than 3,800 tons (3,447 metric tons) of wheat seed to thousands of Afghan farmers in the spring of 2002.

◉ Opium Poppies

Opium poppies, which can be used to make the addictive drugs heroin and opium, have long thrived in eastern Afghanistan. The crops need little water or care and are extremely valuable. Harvested poppies yield raw opium, which is then refined in laboratories in northeastern Afghanistan. Labs in Pakistan also process Afghan poppies into heroin.

Afghanistan has exported drugs to markets in India, Iran, the United States, and Europe. For many years, poppies were the nation's most lucrative commodity, and Afghanistan produced about

In a field near Qandahar, men harvest opium poppies. The poppies will be used for drug production, which has been illegal in Afghanistan since 2001.

three-quarters of the world's opium. The drug traffic was believed to bring the nation as much as $100 million annually. However, Taliban officials banned poppy farming in 2001, putting an end to one of Afghanistan's chief sources of income. Farmers anticipated resuming the business after the Taliban's fall, but international criticism of the drug trade spurred the interim government to reinstate the ban.

Despite the government's work to destroy crops and discourage planting, many impoverished farmers have disobeyed the ban. In August 2002, the United Nations reported that many acres of poppies had survived or been replanted and that a large harvest was expected that year. By October 2002, Afghanistan was once again estimated to be the world's leading producer of poppies.

◉ Mining and Forestry

Although Afghanistan lacks the means to take full advantage of its natural resources, the nation's land does hold valuable materials. Large underground deposits of natural gas exist west of Mazar-e-Sharif, and Afghan governments have been trying to develop drilling facilities in the region since 1967. Fields in Jowzjan Province are already major producers of natural gas, with plants capable of both storing and refining the fuel. However, the conflicts of the late twentieth and early twenty-first centuries have impaired the nation's production ability. By the early 2000s, output had dropped to approximately 22 million cubic feet (622,600 cubic meters) a day—a sharp drop from the peak of about 290 million cubic feet (8.2 million cubic meters) a day during the 1980s.

In addition to natural gas, Afghanistan has proven oil reserves. But, again, ongoing conflicts have prevented progress in drilling and refining. Other natural resources include coal deposits on the northern slopes of the Hindu Kush and in fields in the provinces of Baghlan and Balkh. Afghanistan also has deposits of minerals, such as chromite (from

BEAUTIFUL BLUE

Lapis lazuli, a deep blue semi-precious stone, has been mined in northeastern Afghanistan for more than five thousand years. Artifacts made of Afghan lapis lazuli have been discovered in ancient Sumerian tombs (in present-day Iraq) and in Egyptian burial sites. European painters of the Middle Ages (A.D. 500–A.D. 1500) used ground lapis lazuli as a pigment for skies and seas. With mining centered in the province of Badakhshan, especially within its remote sections in the Hindu Kush, lapis lazuli continues to be one of Afghanistan's most valuable natural resources.

which chrome is made), iron ore, copper, silver, and rock salt. But the country's underdeveloped road network and difficult terrain limit the mining of these reserves.

Forests, another of Afghanistan's resources, are in danger of disappearing. The region was once quite heavily wooded, with most of its natural forests lying in the eastern part of the country and on the south-facing slopes of the Hindu Kush. Stands of evergreens provided wood for the construction industry, while oaks were burned as fuel. Other trees yielded gum resin that was exported to India. Forests of pistachio and other nut trees still provide a reliable product for export, but most of Afghanistan's forestry-related sources of income are dwindling due to over-harvesting for lumber. To prevent further depletion of the country's woods, plans for the future include a national reforestation project.

◉ Industry

Afghanistan's industrial sector remains underdeveloped. Most factories are in Kabul, and production relies on agricultural raw materials that have been hard to transport to the capital during times of war. Many of Afghanistan's factories and plants were built by the Soviet Union or other outside nations, and, without continuing support, they deteriorated during the many years of conflict. Nevertheless, some industries are still in operation. Cotton and woolen textiles, leather goods, furniture, footwear, glass, and cement continue to be among the nation's important manufactured products.

Weavers of traditional handmade items also contribute to production. Hand-knotted wool carpets exported to Iran, Europe, and the United States once earned about 20 percent of Afghanistan's

These Afghan boys help support their families by **dyeing wool.** Visit vgsbooks.com for up-to-date information about Afghanistan's economy and a converter that tells you how many afghanis are in a U.S. dollar.

At this school, Afghan children learn to make colorful wool carpets starting at a young age.

foreign income. Weaving is a largely home-based industry centered in the northern and northwestern provinces. As the Afghan economy struggles to recover, carpet making might once again become a valuable industry.

Transportation and Energy

With few navigable rivers and no railroads, Afghanistan must rely primarily on highways and roads for transportation. Approximately 13,000 miles (20,921 km) of roads crisscross the country. Many of them date back to the 1960s, when the Soviet Union and the United States each funded the construction of highway networks in Afghanistan. But most Afghan roads are in poor repair, and less than 15 percent of them are paved. Bridges are often washed out by flooded rivers. Thousands of commercial vehicles operate in Afghanistan, but rural Afghans still cherish horses as symbols of status and as forms of transport. Camels and donkeys are also commonly used as draft animals.

Afghanistan is one of the few nations in the world that has no national railway. Proposals to build a railway in Afghanistan to link it to its neighbors have been put forth since the 1920s, but none of these

A train of camels approaches the northern town of Aqchah. The animals carry supplies for the town's weekly market.

plans have been carried out. In the early 2000s, Afghan developers began pushing for a similar project.

The nation also hopes to expand its air transportation. Kabul Airport was built with U.S. help in the 1960s and expanded with Soviet aid. Since the Taliban's rise and fall, the United Nations has provided support to rebuild the badly damaged facility. As work proceeds on the airport, the national Afghan airline, Ariana, is resuming domestic and international flights. Service had been interrupted since 1999.

Conflict has severely limited Afghanistan's supply of electricity. Only about 6 percent of the population receive power. Power lines have been damaged, and Kabul still experiences frequent blackouts. Other cities, such as Qandahar and Herat, also suffer electrical shortages and outages. Restoring regular power to the nation's residents is another task facing the new administration.

GETTING CONNECTED

Afghanistan's underdeveloped communications systems got a boost in 2002. A joint study released that year by the World Bank, the Asian Development Bank, and the United Nations Development Programme (UNDP) estimated that there were only two telephones for every one thousand Afghan residents. Starting in April 2002, the Afghan Wireless Communication Company began offering mobile phone service to residents in major cities.

The damming of the Helmand River created a large expanse of **farmland** in the river's valley.

Natural causes have also made Afghanistan's power supply unreliable. Most of the nation's energy is provided by hydroelectric plants, and several dams harness the Helmand and Kabul Rivers. However, drought and other seasonal shifts in water flow hinder the rivers' energy potential. Many of the hydropower stations between Kabul and Jalalabad and in the provinces are badly in need of repair. The rest of Afghanistan's electricity comes from coal, thermal power (heat energy from fossil fuels), and imported oil.

The Future

Afghanistan's economic development still lags far behind that of most of the world's countries. But in the early years of the twenty-first century, the nation faces a future filled with both uncertainty and possibility. Following the ouster of the Taliban, the new government has, at least temporarily, resolved much of the country's internal conflict. Foreign powers around the world have pledged their aid to Afghanistan as the country rebuilds and recovers from decades of war. Hundreds of thousands of refugees and emigrants are streaming home, eager to contribute to their nation's future.

However, even as Afghans look ahead to new and brighter prospects, the country continues to encounter a host of major hurdles. For example, warlords in the provinces still present a threat to stability. Longstanding rivalries among these provincial leaders are hard to eliminate, and the government in Kabul finds it especially difficult to enforce law and order in rural Afghanistan. In addition to these ongoing security concerns, the funds that are so badly needed to rebuild the country have been harder to receive than anticipated. While many nations promised aid to Afghanistan after the conflict of the early 2000s, not all of these countries have followed through with their pledges. Without these funds, Afghan leaders worry, the nation could slip back into turmoil.

> "In this critical time, when our motherland is watching our actions, let us come together and be brothers and sisters. Let us be good to each other and be compassionate and share our grief. Let us forget the sad past."
>
> —Hamid Karzai

Further blows to the country came in July 2002, when U.S. forces mistakenly identified a village as a Taliban holdout and bombed the area, killing and injuring dozens of civilians. Later that same month, Haji Abdul Qadir, a cabinet minister and vice president in President Karzai's administration, was assassinated. Observers speculated that the killing may have been related to the struggling opium trade. Karzai himself survived an assassination attempt on September 5, 2002, but a bomb exploded in a Kabul bazaar that same day, killing and wounding dozens of people. Other violence has included attacks on girls' schools, carried out by a group claiming to support the Taliban's ban on the education of girls and women.

Each setback illustrates the difficult path that lies before Afghanistan's leaders as they strive to establish a strong and secure government. Safety, health, and education are short-term priorities. Striking a balance between the nation's strong Islamic and cultural traditions and its role in a modern global community will be another important step.

There are many challenges ahead. But Afghans have proven to be a strong and resilient people. Despite the obstacles, they are hopeful that their ancient and often troubled nation will soon find the peace and stability that it has sought for years.

CA. 8000 B.C.	People begin settling in the region that will become Afghanistan.
CA. 1500 B.C.	Bactrians inhabit urban centers in Bactria.
CA. 330 B.C.	Alexander the Great conquers Bactria.
CA. 100S B.C.	The Kushan spread Buddhism in Afghanistan.
A.D. 78–103	Kaniska rules the region.
CA. 600S	Muslim armies bring Islam to Afghanistan.
1186	Ghurid troops overthrow the Ghaznavids.
1220	Mongol armies invade Afghanistan.
1380	Timur conquers northern Afghanistan.
1405	The Timurid dynasty is founded and supports the arts in Afghanistan.
CA. 1494–1530	Babur writes the *Baburnama*, his memoirs.
1747	Nader Shah is assassinated and Ahmad Shah Durrani becomes king.
1773	Ahmad Shah dies and Timur Shah becomes king.
1826	Dost Mohammad Khan takes control of Kabul.
1839–1842	First Anglo-Afghan War is fought.
1863	Shir Ali Khan takes the throne.
1878–1879	Second Anglo-Afghan War is fought.
1893	The Durand Line is established between Afghanistan and Pakistan.
1907	Russia and Britain sign the Anglo-Russian Convention.
1914–1918	World War I is fought.
1919	Third Anglo-Afghan War is fought.
1923	Amanollah Khan enacts an Afghan constitution.
1925	Radio Kabul (later Radio Afghanistan) begins broadcasts.
1932	Kabul University is founded.
1933	Mohammad Zahir Shah takes the throne.
1934	Afghanistan joins the League of Nations.
1939–1945	World War II is fought.

1961   Pakistan and Afghanistan break diplomatic relations with each other.

1973   Sardar Mohammad Daud Khan leads a coup to depose King Zahir Shah and sets up a republic.

1977   Women's rights activist Meena founds the Revolutionary Association of the Women of Afghanistan (RAWA).

1978   The People's Democratic Party of Afghanistan (PDPA) establishes the Democratic Republic of Afghanistan.

1979   Soviet troops enter Afghanistan and civil war begins.

1980   Afghan musician Farhad Darya performs on television, beginning a successful career.

1989   Soviet troops complete their retreat from Afghanistan.

1992   Burhanuddin Rabbani is named acting president of the Islamic State of Afghanistan.

1993   The mujahideen sign a peace agreement with each other.

1996   The Taliban captures Kabul.

1997   The Taliban establishes the Islamic Emirate of Afghanistan.

1998   Severe earthquakes hit Afghanistan. U.S. bombings target terrorist training camps in Afghanistan.

2001   The Taliban destroys the Buddhas of Bamian. Ahmad Shah Massoud is assassinated. Terrorist attacks linked to Osama bin Laden, who has been sheltered by Afghanistan, strike the World Trade Center and the Pentagon in the United States. An international offensive led by the United States helps defeat the Taliban, and an interim government is established under Hamid Karzai.

2002   An emergency loya jirga elects President Hamid Karzai, who survives an assassination attempt later in the year. In October, the Central Afghanistan Bank issues currency to boost the afghani's value.

COUNTRY NAME Islamic State of Afghanistan

AREA 251,773 square miles (652,092 sq. km)

MAIN LANDFORMS Hindu Kush, Khyber Pass, Rigestan Desert, Wakhan Corridor

HIGHEST POINT Nowshak Peak, 24,551 feet (7,483 m) above sea level

LOWEST POINT Amu Darya, 846 feet (258 m) above sea level

MAJOR RIVERS Kabul, Amu Darya, Helmand, Hari Rud

ANIMALS Markhor sheep, gazelles, Afghan foxes, snow leopards, brown bears, Asiatic black bears, cranes, herons, pheasants, partridges, pigeons

CAPITAL CITY Kabul

OTHER MAJOR CITIES Herat, Mazar-e-Sharif, Qandahar, Jalalabad

OFFICIAL LANGUAGES Dari and Pashto

MONETARY UNIT Afghani

Currency   Fast Facts

AFGHAN CURRENCY

Afghans buy and sell with afghanis, the country's national currency. Some afghani bills were printed by the Rabbani government in the early 1990s and later used by the Taliban. Others were printed in Russia under the direction of the Northern Alliance. The printing of large numbers of bills throughout the civil war led to a drastic devaluing of the afghani, which in 2002 was estimated to be worth approximately one-seven-hundredth of its former value. To strengthen the currency, Afghanistan's central bank issued new afghanis in 2002. Each new afghani was worth one thousand old afghanis.

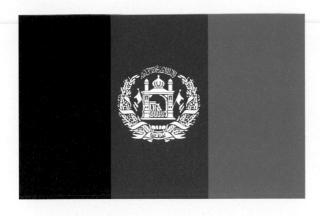

Each regime that has held power throughout Afghanistan's history has flown its own flag. From 1996 to 2001, the nation had two flags. One represented the Rabbani government and the Northern Alliance, and the other represented the Taliban. In June 2002, Hamid Karzai's government officially adopted a new flag. Based on the flag of King Zahir Shah's reign, the standard is a tricolor with vertical bands of black, red, and green. Upon the center band a crest shows a mosque surrounded by a wreath of wheat. Arabic script above the mosque says, "There is no God but Allah and Muhammad is the Prophet of Allah" and "God is Almighty."

Afghanistan's national anthem, like its flag, changed with the inauguration of the new post-Taliban government. The former anthem, "Sououd-e-Melli," had been officially adopted by Sardar Mohammad Daud Khan's administration in 1978. In late 2001, the interim government organized the recording of a new national anthem. The new song was performed at Karzai's first inauguration ceremony in 2002. An English translation of one of the anthem's verses follows:

Afghan National Anthem
Live happy, live free, and live prosperous
O motherland in the light of God's law
The torch of freedom shall be the vision to the bewildered people.

God is great, God is great.

For a link to a website where you can listen to Afghanistan's new national anthem, go to vgsbooks.com.

AHMAD SHAH DURRANI (ca. 1722–1793) Born in Herat, Ahmad Shah was the son of a tribal chief and grew up to become an important leader himself. In 1747, after the death of Persian king Nader Shah, Pashtun chiefs chose Ahmad as shah. He went on to conquer territory in northern and eastern Afghanistan, as well as large regions of India. Under Ahmad's rule, Afghanistan was, for the first time, a united nation. For that achievement, he is remembered as the founder of the nation and its first ruler.

AHMAD SHAH MASSOUD (ca. 1953–2001) Massoud was born in the Panjshir Valley, north of Kabul. Massoud studied engineering, but when Soviet forces invaded in 1979 he emerged as a skillful and charismatic leader of the mujahideen. After the Soviet withdrawal, Massoud became Rabbani's minister of defense. Bitter fighting continued among ethnic and religious groups, and Massoud's forces frequently clashed with those of rival leader Gulbuddin Hekmatyar. With the rise of the Taliban, Massoud returned to Panjshir and helped establish the Northern Alliance, a resistance group against the new regime. In 2001 Massoud was killed by assassins posing as journalists.

BABUR (1483–1530) Although he originally came from Fergana, a region in present-day Uzbekistan, Babur, whose given name was Zahir-ud-Din Muhammed, became deeply attached to Kabul after capturing the city in 1504. A descendant of both Timur and Genghis Khan, Babur became king of Fergana when he was twelve years old. Although he lost Fergana to rivals, he was a strong leader who eventually founded the Moghul Empire in India. In addition to his military and political pursuits, Babur was a poet and writer. His memoirs, the *Baburnama*, offer detailed observations of the lands to which he traveled. Babur was buried, at his request, in Bagh-i-Babur, a garden in Kabul.

RABIA BALKHI (?–940) Balkhi, born in the village of Balkh, is remembered as the first woman to write poetry in the Persian language. Balkhi wrote passionate love poems and, according to legend, died tragically when she was killed for having a love affair with a slave. Balkhi's tomb, located in Balkh, is visited by young people who come to ask for good fortune in their love affairs. Balkhi is also the namesake of Kabul's Rabia Balkhi Women's Hospital.

FARHAD DARYA (b. 1962) Darya is a popular musician who grew up in the province of Konduz. In 1979 he moved to Kabul, where he studied at the university and eventually became a professor of classical music. Darya also joined a band, which became the orchestra for the national radio and television stations. Darya left Afghanistan in 1990 and resides in the United States, but his music is still very popular in his homeland. Darya's songs are greatly influenced by Afghan traditions, and many of them include political statements. After the Taliban's fall, Darya's popular song "Beloved Kabul" was broadcast on Radio Afghanistan.

HAMID KARZAI (b. 1957) Karzai was born in Qandahar. He was the son of a prominent Pashtun leader and the cousin of then-king Zahir Shah. After the Soviet invasion in 1979, Karzai's family left for Pakistan, and Karzai went on to study in India. He later split his time between Afghanistan and Pakistan. He served in Rabbani's government for two years but left the country during the Taliban's reign. After the September 11 attacks on the United States, Karzai returned to Afghanistan to support the anti-Taliban resistance. He became the leader of the interim government in December 2001, and he was chosen as the nation's new president in June 2002.

KHALILULLAH KHALILI (1907–1987) Born in Kabul, Khalili is commonly known as Afghanistan's poet laureate. He studied classical literature and went on to publish many works of poetry, fiction, and history. Khalili lectured at Kabul University and also became involved in the government. He was appointed minister of press and information for King Zahir Shah in 1951. Khalili later served as a member of Parliament and as the Afghan ambassador to Saudi Arabia and Iraq.

MEENA (1957–1987) Born in Kabul, Meena was a prominent women's rights activist. In 1977 she formed the Revolutionary Association of the Women of Afghanistan (RAWA). RAWA is an organization dedicated to securing rights for Afghan women and to giving them a voice in the nation's society and government. In 1981 Meena began publishing *Payam-e-Zan (Women's Message)*, a magazine that promoted RAWA's goals. Some of RAWA's accomplishments were to set up schools for refugee children and to provide employment opportunities to women. In 1987 Meena was killed in Pakistan. RAWA members believe that Meena's assassins were members of the Afghan branch of the Soviet secret service.

MOHAMMAD ZAHIR SHAH (b. 1914) Zahir Shah, the son of the Pashtun king Muhammad Nader Khan, attended schools in Kabul and France as a youth. When his father was assassinated in 1933, Zahir Shah became king at the age of nineteen. The young king was initially guided by his powerful family, but in 1963 he forced his cousin Sardar Mohammad Daud Khan from his post as prime minister and began to exercise greater power of his own. In 1964 Zahir Shah put a new constitution into effect that created a more democratic and modern form of government. However, Daud deposed the king and regained power in 1973. Zahir Shah lived in exile in Italy for twenty-nine years before returning to Afghanistan as a supporter of leader Hamid Karzai in the post-Taliban nation.

Afghanistan has a long history and a landscape of striking natural beauty. While these qualities give the country many interesting sights to visit in times of peace, instability still renders Afghanistan a risky destination for tourists. Anyone considering going to Afghanistan should check with the U.S. State Department (see the website at <http://travel.state.gov/travel_warnings.html>) and with embassies in Afghanistan to determine the safety of travel in the region.

BAND-I-AMIR Located about 45 miles (72 km) west of Bamian, the mountain lakes of Band-i-Amir are situated among dramatic cliffs. The five lakes are connected by natural dams over which waterfalls spill, and they are noted for their exceptionally clear, blue water.

BLUE MOSQUE The Blue Mosque in Mazar-e-Sharif is considered one of the most sacred Islamic sites in Afghanistan. It is believed to hold the tomb of Ali, the cousin and son-in-law of the prophet Muhammad. Also known as the "Tomb of the Chosen One," the mosque is a place of pilgrimage for Muslims from all over Afghanistan and beyond.

CHIHIL ZINA This unique attraction, dating to about the time of Babur's reign in the 1500s, lies outside Qandahar. Forty steps, carved from the face of a cliff, lead to a small stone chamber guarded by stone lions. The chamber contains inscriptions describing Qandahar, its history, and Babur's accomplishments. At the end of the climb, visitors can enjoy a splendid view of Qandahar and the surrounding plains.

KABUL Once a bustling center of commerce, Kabul is coming alive again as peace returns. Shoppers at the bazaar may purchase items from hats to chess sets, and carpet sellers display their handwoven wares on sidewalks and in parks. Hungry visitors can stop at restaurants for freshly prepared Afghan meals. Also located in and around Kabul are structures built during Amanollah Khan's reign (1919–1929). These include a victory arch built after the final defeat of the British in 1919, and the massive Darulaman Palace, built in 1923 as the king's residence. Both of these structures have been damaged by many years of war.

MINARET OF JAM One of Afghanistan's ancient treasures, the Minaret of Jam stands in a remote valley more than 100 miles (161 km) east of Herat. At 213 feet (65 m) high, this intricately carved and decorated pillar is the second-tallest minaret in the world. It is also one of the oldest, dating back to the Ghurid era of the late 1100s and early 1200s.

SHAHR-I-GHOLGOLA Shahr-i-Gholgola, or "City of Sighs," was the site of a fierce and bloody battle against Genghis Khan's invading armies in 1222. The city's residents were massacred and its buildings were demolished. One watchtower stands amid the ruins atop a cliff overlooking Bamian's valley, where the great Buddha statues once stood.

Buddhism: a religion founded in India by the philosopher and monk Siddhartha Gautama (Buddha). Buddhism gained a following in China around the fourth and fifth centuries A.D. Some of Buddhism's ideals are the search for enlightenment, the renouncement of worldly things, and a life of virtue and wisdom.

Communism: a political and economic model based on the idea of common, rather than private property. In a Communist system, the government controls capital and distributes it equally among citizens. The ideas of Communism are very similar to those of Socialism.

Islam: a religion founded on the Arabian Peninsula in the seventh century A.D. by the prophet Muhammad. The religion's primary tenets are known as the Five Pillars of Islam. Most followers of Islam, called Muslims, are members of the Sunni sect, while others follow the Shiite branch of the religion. Nearly all Afghans are Muslims.

khan: a ruler or tribal leader in Afghanistan. Khans, such as Genghis Khan of the Mongols, also led people in China and other Asian nations.

mujahideen: Afghan resistance fighters. The mujahideen fought the Soviets during their occupation of Afghanistan (1979–1989). During the Taliban's reign, some members of the mujahideen joined the United National and Islamic Front for the Salvation of Afghanistan, also called the Northern Alliance, to fight the new regime. Most mujahideen are devout Muslims.

opium poppies: a variety of poppy that yields the addictive drug opium. Opium itself can be further refined to produce other drugs, such as heroin and morphine. Opium poppies thrive in hot, dry climates, and they have been a profitable crop in Afghanistan for many years.

Persia: the ancient region that became Iran. The language spoken in Iran and western Afghanistan is still called Persian.

Quran: the holy book of Islam. According to Islamic belief, the Quran's teachings were communicated by Allah (God) to the prophet Muhammad. These divine messages were later collected and recorded in a single volume, written in Arabic.

shah: a ruler, often of an Islamic society. The word *shah* is added to a ruler's name when that person assumes the throne. (For example, Ahmad Khan became Ahmad Shah.)

Sharia: Islamic law. Most of the rules of Sharia are derived from the Quran, but various Muslim sects and governments interpret and apply Sharia differently. Under the Taliban, Sharia punishments could be harsh. For example, a person convicted of stealing would have his or her hand cut off, while a person found guilty of adultery might be publicly stoned to death.

Selected Bibliography

Adamec, Ludwig W. *Historical Dictionary of Afghanistan.* Lanham, MD: The Scarecrow Press, Inc., 1997.
This reference book provides concise information on a wide range of Afghan history and culture.

"Afghanistan: The Latest." *ReliefWeb.* 2002.
<http://www.reliefweb.int/w/rwb.nsf/ByCountry/Afghanistan?OpenDocument&StartKey=Afghanistan&Expandview> (June 12, 2002).
This site, representing a United Nations program, presents current news articles and reports about Afghanistan from a diverse selection of sources.

"Afghanistan: News, Information and Pictures." *UK Committee for Unicef.* N.d.
<http://www.unicef.org.uk/news/index.htm> (June 12, 2002).
Part of the United Kingdom's branch of the United Nations Children's Fund, this site presents news and background information on Afghanistan and UNICEF's work there.

Babur, Emperor of Hindustan. *The Baburnama: Memoirs of Babur, Prince and Emperor.* Translated and edited by Wheeler M. Thackston. New York: Oxford University Press, 1996.
Babur's memoirs offer readers a unique glimpse of Afghanistan through the eyes of a conqueror.

Cable News Network. *CNN.com Asia.* 2002.
<http://asia.cnn.com> (June 12, 2002).
This site provides current events and breaking news about Afghanistan, as well as a searchable archive of older articles.

Dupree, Louis. *Afghanistan.* Princeton, NJ: Princeton University Press, 1973.
Considered one of the most important histories ever written of Afghanistan, Dupree's classic work offers readers information about the land, the people, and the history of the country.

Europa World Yearbook, 2001. Vol. II. London: Europa Publications, 2001.
Covering Afghanistan's recent history, economy, and government, this annual publication also provides a wealth of statistics on population, employment, trade, and more.

Ewans, Sir Martin. *Afghanistan: A Short History of Its People and Politics.* New York: HarperCollins Publishers, 2002.
This concise volume presents an overview of Afghan history.

New York Times Company. *The New York Times on the Web.* 2002.
<www.nytimes.com> (July 15, 2002).
This online version of the newspaper offers current news stories along with an archive of articles on Afghanistan.

"PRB 2001 World Population Data Sheet." *Population Reference Bureau (PRB).* 2001.
<http://www.prb.org> (June 12, 2002).
This annual statistics sheet provides data on Afghanistan's population, birth and death rates, fertility rate, infant mortality rate, and other information.

Rowland, Benjamin. *Art in Afghanistan: Objects from the Kabul Museum.* With photographs by Frances Mortimer Rice. London: The Penguin Press, 1971.
This volume presents dozens of photographs of Afghan art and artifacts, accompanied by informative text.

Saberi, Helen. *Afghan Food and Cookery.* New York: Hippocrene Books, Inc., 2000.
This cookbook introduces readers to the delicious cuisine of Afghanistan.

Turner, Barry, ed. *The Statesman's Yearbook: The Politics, Cultures, and Economies of the World, 2002.* New York: Macmillan Press, 2001.
This resource provides concise information on Afghan history, climate, government, economy, and culture, including relevant statistics.

UNESCO. *Unesco and Afghanistan.* 2002.
<http://portal.unesco.org/ev.php?URL_ID=1259&URL_DO=DO_TOPIC&URL_SEC-TION=201> (June 12, 2002).
Run by the United Nations Educational, Scientific and Cultural Organization, this site provides information related to UNESCO's efforts to help reconstruct Afghanistan.

USAID: Humanitarian Crisis in Central Asia. N.d.
<http://www.usaid.gov/about/afghanistan> (June 12, 2002).
Run by the United States Agency for International Development, this site publishes articles and reports on aid in Afghanistan.

World Bank Group. *The World Bank in Afghanistan.* 2002.
<http://lnweb18.worldbank.org/sar/sa.nsf/Afghanistan> (June 12, 2002).
This site provides information on the World Bank's activities in Afghanistan.

World Health Organization. *World Health Organization.* 2001.
<http://www.who.int/home-page> (June 12, 2002).
The official homepage of the World Health Organization provides information and updates on health topics in Afghanistan and around the world.

Afgha.com Press Agency.
Website: <http://www.afgha.com>
This informative website provides news, photos, downloads, and links related to Afghanistan.

Afghanistan Online.
Website: <http://www.afghan-web.com>
This extensive site offers a wealth of information on Afghan culture, arts, and history.

Afghan Music MP3.
Website: <http://www.afghanan.net/music>
Visit this site to listen to hundreds of Afghan songs—popular, classical, vocal, and instrumental—in addition to readings of Pashto poetry.

Corona, Laurel. *Afghanistan.* **San Diego: Lucent Books, 2002.**
This book provides an overview of Afghanistan's geography and history, along with information on modern life and culture.

Elliot, Jason. *An Unexpected Light: Travels in Afghanistan.* **New York: Picador USA, 1999.**
This travel narrative offers an inside glimpse of life in Afghanistan.

Ellis, Deborah. *The Breadwinner.* **Berkeley, CA: Publishers Group West, 2001.**
This novel tells the story of a young girl living in Afghanistan during the Taliban's rule.

Gritzner, Jeffrey A. *Afghanistan.* **Philadelphia: Chelsea House Publishers, 2002.**
This book provides an overview of Afghanistan's geography, history, and society.

Lemar-Aftaab.
Website: <http://www.afghanmagazine.com>
This online magazine publishes articles on Afghan art, culture, society, and people.

Lessing, Doris. *The Wind Blows Away Our Words.* **New York: Vintage Books, 1987.**
Lessing's work depicts the life of Afghan refugees living in Pakistan.

Nye, Naomi Shihab. *Nineteen Varieties of Gazelle: Poems of the Middle East.* **New York: Greenwillow Books, 2002.**
This volume of poetry offers readers insight into Islam, life in the Middle East (usually defined as southwestern and central Asia, which includes Afghanistan, and northeastern Africa), and the experience of being an Arab American.

Penney, Sue. *Islam.* **Chicago: Heinemann Library, 2000.**
Readers are introduced to Islam, the religion of nearly all Afghan people.

Further Reading and Websites

Shah, Idries. *The Magic Horse.* **Cambridge, MA: Hoopoe Books, 1998.**
This colorfully illustrated picture book presents an old tale, retold by Afghan writer Idries Shah.

vgsbooks.com
Website: <http://www.vgsbooks.com>
Visit vgsbooks.com, the homepage of the Visual Geography Series®. You can get linked to all sorts of useful on-line information, including geographical, historical, demographic, cultural, and economic websites. The vgsbooks.com site is a great resource for late-breaking news and statistics.

Zoya. *Zoya's Story: An Afghan Woman's Struggle for Freedom.* **New York: William Morrow, 2002.**
Born in 1979, Zoya grew up amid the conflict and turmoil of Afghanistan in the 1980s and 1990s. In this book, she tells her story with detail and emotion.

Index

League of Nations, 26
legal system, 37
literacy, 43
literature, 49
livestock, 57–58

malnutrition, 45
maps, 7, 11
Margow Desert, 12
Massoud, Ahmad Shah. *See* Ahmad
  Shah Massoud
Mazar-e-Sharif, 17, 35
mining, 60–61
Mongol Empire, 21
mountains, 9–10
mujahideen, 5–6, 29–32, 34
music and dance, 52
Muslims, 5, 30, 46–47, 51

Nader Khan, Muhammad, 26
Najibullah, 31, 32
national anthem, 69
natural gas, 60
Northern Alliance, 33–35
Nowshak Peak, 10
Nuristanis, 39, 41

Omar, Mullah Mohammed, 32
opium poppies, 59–60

Pakistan, 6, 8, 10, 27–28, 30–32, 38
Parcham, 28–29
Paropamisus Mountains, 9–10, 13
Pashtuns, 22, 27, 32–33, 36, 39–40
people, 38–45: education, 42–43;
  ethnic groups, 39–41; health,
  43–45; language, 41–42
People's Democratic Party of
  Afghanistan (PDPA), 28–29
Persian Empire, 18–20
Plateau of Iran, 12
population, 38

al-Qaeda, 33–35
Qandahar, 16, 19, 23, 24, 53

Rabbani, Burhanuddin, 31–33
Radio Afghanistan, 52
Rahman Khan, Abdor, 25
rainfall, 14–15

recreation, 52–53
refugees, 30–31, 38, 64
religion, 46–47
Rigestan Desert, 12
rivers, 12–13
Russia, 24–26

Safed Koh Range, 10
Second Anglo-Afghan War, 25
Seleucid dynasty, 19–20
Shiites, 47
Shir Ali Khan, 25, 42
Shoja, Shah, 24–25
Silk Road, 20
Soviet Union, 6, 27–31, 34, 42, 61, 62
Sunnis, 47

Tajikistan, 8, 10, 12
Tajiks, 39–40
Taliban, 4, 6, 32–35, 38, 42–44,
  48–49, 52, 54–55, 60, 63, 64–65
Taraki, Nur Mohammad, 28–29
terrorism, 33–34
Third Anglo-Afghan War, 26, 48
Timur, 21–22
topography, 8–12
transportation, 62–63
Turkmenistan, 8–9, 13, 42
Turkomans, 39–40, 42

United National and Islamic Front
  for the Salvation of Afghanistan
  (UNIFSA), 33
United Nations (UN), 31, 45
United Nations Educational,
  Scientific and Cultural
  Organization (UNESCO), 43
United States, 27–29, 33–34, 62, 63
Uzbekistan, 8–9, 12, 42
Uzbeks, 39–40, 42

visual arts, 53–55

Wakhan Corridor, 8, 10, 20
women, 26, 27, 28, 30, 42–43, 65
World Trade Center attacks, 33–34

Zahir Shah, Mohammad, 26–28, 35–36
Zahir-ud-Din Muhammad (Babur),
  14, 22

Captions for photos appearing on cover and chapter openers:

Cover: The Friday Mosque in Herat features detailed tilework.

pp. 4–5 Traders gather in the northern Afghanistan village of Balkh.

pp. 8–9 A small town lies between mountains and the Kabul River.

pp. 38–39 A group of Afghan men linger at a *chai khana,* or teahouse.

pp. 46–47 The Blue Mosque in Mazar-e-Sharif is thought to contain the tomb of Ali, a relative of the prophet Muhammad.

pp. 56–57 Spice merchants display their goods at a market in Jalalabad.

Photo Acknowledgments
The images in this book are used with the permission of: © TRIP/R. Zampese, pp. 4–5, 61; PresentationMaps.com, pp. 7, 11; © John Elk III, pp. 8–9, 14, 15, 17, 38–39, 46–47, 63; © TRIP/M. Lines, pp. 10, 16, 56–57; © TRIP/J. Skellron, p. 12; © Reuters NewMedia Inc./CORBIS, pp. 13, 36, 68; © North Wind Pictures, p. 21; © Stapleton Collection/CORBIS, p. 23; © National Army Museum, London, p. 24; © Tate Gallery, London/Art Resource, NY, p. 25; © Hulton-Deutsch Collection/CORBIS, p. 27 (top); © Hulton Archive_Getty Images, pp. 27 (bottom), 31; © Associated Press, pp. 28, 59; U.S. Department of State, p. 29; © TRIP/Trip, pp. 30, 41; © Patrick Robert/CORBIS Sygma, p. 32; © AFP/CORBIS, pp. 33, 34, 35 (top); © U.S. Agency for International Development, p. 35 (bottom); © Gunes Kocatepe/Atlas Geographic, pp. 40, 53; Defense Link/U.S. Department of Defense, p. 43; © Jack A. Hill, p. 44; M. Griffin/FAO, pp. 45, 58; © TRIP/C. Watmough, p. 49; © TRIP/H. Leonard, p. 51; © Daniel H. Condit, p. 54; FAO, p. 62; © Carl & Ann Purcell/CORBIS, p. 64; Laura Westlund, p. 69.

Cover photo: © Scala/Art Resource, NY. Back cover photo: NASA.